Cooverjee Sorabjee Nazir

The first Parsee Barone:

Being passages from the life and fortunes of the late Sir Jamsetjee

Jeejeebhoy Baronet

Cooverjee Sorabjee Nazir

The first Parsee Barone:
Being passages from the life and fortunes of the late Sir Jamsetjee Jeejeebhoy Baronet

ISBN/EAN: 9783337714987

Printed in Europe, USA, Canada, Australia, Japan

Cover: Foto ©ninafisch / pixelio.de

More available books at **www.hansebooks.com**

THE FIRST PARSEE BÁRONET,

BEING

PASSAGES

FROM THE LIFE AND FORTUNES

OF

THE LATE

SIR JAMSETJEE JEEJEEBHOY BARONET.

BY

COOVERJEE SORABJEE NAZIR,

Late Junior Scholar, Elphinstone College, Bombay.

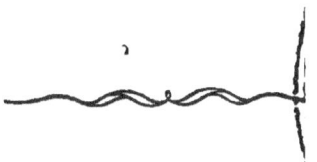

BOMBAY:
PRINTED AT THE UNION PRESS

1866.

PREFACE.

"Le *moi* est haissable," says a distinguished Frenchman, but he might have added that the use of "little i with a dot" is unfortunately not always to be avoided even with the best intention to be retiring. To write a preface, at the request of the author, for another man's book, is a somewhat difficult, although withal a flattering task, inasmuch as the writer of the preface is expected to act as guide to the pages which follow, and has the pleasing conviction to comfort himself with that the very ideas and motives which he credits to his author may prove exactly what the author never intended ; while the author is then placed in the dilemma of either declining the preface and offending his friend, or of sending forth his book into the world under false colours. But as the worthy Mrs Lirriper observes, Gentle Public, "you will take as you find."

Happily the days are gone by when the book sold solely through the merit of the preface, and the preface constituted more than a fair share of the entire volume, or the author of the following *brochure*, as he modestly terms his memoir, would fare but ill. He has indeed left so little to be said in the preface, that there is hardly any need for such an encumbrance, since the introductory chapter of his book is exhaustive in itself. This however may be the fittest place for acknowledging the source whence the following "Life" drew its birth, as it is nowhere mentioned in the work itself. A poem by one "Munsookh," whose name will be familiar to Native readers, upon Sir Jamsetjee Jeejeebhoy, composed not long after his death, has been taken as the groundwork of the memoir, the first three chapters being taken almost entirely from the poem. It was found, however, as the work progressed, that the epithets and phraseology which abound in the poem were unsuited to a prose work, and the author has written on in his own style, referring only to "Munsookh's" composition for facts unattainable elsewhere.

The apparent anachronism in the body of this work, where the arrival of Jamsetjee's patent of Knighthood is mentioned after it had been stated that a Baronetcy was conferred upon him is accounted for by the author, on the ground that he considered it better to narrate the history of Jamsetjee's charities in a connected form, than to intersperse it with the story of his life.

It must be a matter of congratulation, to all, that the failure which has to be deplored in some instances has not been imitated in the case of Sir Jamsetjee Jeejeebhoy. True it is that

> The world knows nothing of its greatest men;

but it is painful as it is extraordinary that some of the world's greatest benefactors should have been permitted to pass not only from the scene of their worth, but almost into the remote past with their history comparatively unnoticed, while record *usque ad nauseam* has been preserved of those it were well we could forget. Slender though this little memoir be, and from a maiden pen, it will be read, and read with deep interest by all who knew and esteemed its subject, and be perused where a fuller biography might remain unread and unappreciated. It is a simple narrative, told in a simple way, with an evident sense of the worth of a departed friend. Of the style, the reader must judge for himself.

It should be borne in mind however that the author was unable to complete his course of study at the Elphinstone College, and he is therefore worthy of greater indulgence, as writing in a foreign language with far from efficient preparation to cope with its manifold difficulties.

It is difficult to write a readable biography of a man whose chief aim in life was the acquisition of wealth, and whose sole desire in his prosperous days was to do as much good as he could with it, but we believe the author has made the best of his subject. At any rate the literature of Young India would have been incomplete without a life of the man who was so perfect a master of the art of speculation that he was able by one stroke of business to realize a splendid profit of fortyfive lakhs of Rupees, an almost incredible feat, but who at the same time was

PREFACE. ix

capable of at any moment putting the curb
upon his spirit of adventures.

> A little luck, a little keen address,
> A little kindly help in time of need,
> A little industry and touch of greed,
> Have made his life a singular success;

but happily the "touch of greed" never developed into avarice, and his open handed liberality has passed almost into a proverb.

I should not, I hope, be trespassing on my friend's ground if I here relate an anecdote concerning the late Baronet, which is current among the Parsee Community, and which if not actually true, might very well be so. *Quantum valeat*, here it is. When Jamsetjee first went to China with his relative Mr. Merwanjee Tuback, he was one day weighing out opium, in which interesting occupation he was observed by what would in these days (what time Dean Alford's influence reigneth not,) a "constituent" of the firm, who was evidently a Lavater in his way. "Ah"! exclaimed he,* "that young man will one day become a very rich merchant, and his present master will become

---
* note a la Dr. Marigold. I never opened a book yet without finding that individuals similar to the above always "exclaim", and invariably commence with "ah"!

his servant", which prediction strangely enough was actually verified.

I hope I have said enough and not too much to satisfy the requirements of my friend. I have indeed been led to write more than the few words I originally intended to prefix to his little volume. But I owe him a few words of apology. In correcting his proofs as they went through the press, I have frequently, owing to my own duties, caused him unavoidable, and, I fear, sometimes vexatious delay. His persecutions by "devils" for "copy" appear to have almost equalled the attacks upon the good St. Anthony. But now, he has all his copy and all his preface, "at larst," as the lady exclaimed to Mr. Artemus Ward, "at larst, oh! at larst."

MATTHEW HENRY SCOTT, C. S.

Surat, 10th March, 1866.

CONTENTS.

CHAPTER I.
                                            PAGE.

Parentage—Sir Jamsetjee's birth—early clouds. . . . . 1— 4

CHAPTER II.
The "Reaper, whose name is death"—A father's advice—Orphanage. . . . . 4— 7

CHAPTER III.
Goes to Bombay—Enters the service of Mr. Framjee Bottlewalla—Whose daughter he marries—The Marriage ceremonies—the rejoicings. . . . . 7— 12

CHAPTER IV.
He emerges into manhood—Goes to China—Second voyage to China—a prospect of danger—The engagement—After the Battle—A Dance—Returns to Bombay. . 12— 18

CHAPTER V.
His last visit to China—His ship captured by the French—He is landed at the Cape—Hard times—a "ministering angel"—Arrival in Calcutta—Reflections. 18— 23

CHAPTER VI.
Arrival at home—Friends reunited—"I would he were here"—"*Domi manet*"—

His mercantile genius—His partners—
"Sweet are the uses of adversity"—Independence—Charity, its standard. . . . 23— 30

CHAPTER VII.

Gifts of charity—Payment of debts of men in the Civil gaol—Surat Agiary rebuilt — The Ghambar Fund—Disastrous Fire in Surat—He aids the poor—The Mahim Causeway—Government undertakes the project—it fails—Jamsetjee comes to the rescue—Description of the causeway—The opening ceremony—The Governor's Speech—Lady Jamsetjee's proposal—Ressponse of the Court of Directors—Jamsetjee's speech—The Bund at Poona—The *Ulie Bag*—The Dharamsala at Khandalla—The Dharamsala at Byculla—The first Hospital in Bombay—Jamsetjee's proposal to build an Hospital—Government consents—Laying the First stone—The first masonic display in Bombay—The procession of masons—The ceremony—Inscription on the Plate—The laying of the stone—Masonic addresses—Dr. Burne's address—Conclusion of the speech—Jamsetjee's reply—Educational projects—Advantages of Education—School Fund established—A poor fund for Surat and Nowsari—Miscellaneous contributions to worthy objects—The school of arts—"Deeds above heroic." . 30— 72

CHAPTER VIII.

A grateful recognition—Jamsetjee Knighted—The despatch—The ceremony—The Governor's speech—Jamsetjee's reply—Congratulations.. . . . . 72— 80

CHAPTER IX.

Address of congratulation by the Native Friends of Jamsetjee—The testimonial—An agreeable surprise—Mr. Framjee Cowasjee's address—The address—Growing opinion of India—Allusions to Jamsetjee's munificence—Guzerati Translation Fund formed—Address from Poona, Nugger, Sattara, Jalna, Ahmednugger and Hyderabad—Sir Jamsetjee's reply—Sir Jamsetjee's coat of arms. . . . . . . 80— 93

CHAPTER X.

A proposal to erect a statue to Sir Jamsetjee—a meeting is called in Bombay—Lord Elphinstone's Speech—Mr. Anderson's speech—The proposal carried out. 93—107

CHAPTER XI.

A Baronetcy conferred upon Jamsetjee. He endows his posterity—A special act passed for the purpose. . . . . 107—109

CHAPTER XII.

Jamsetjee's domestic life—His three sons—Cursetjee, Rustomjee and Sorabjee—His daughter Bae Pherozbae—His approaching end—Death scene. . . . . . . 109—113

CHAPTER XIII.

Sir Jamsetjee's character. . . . . . . 114—115.

This book belongs to Rattanjee Vicajee Balsa

The first Parsee Baronet.

ERRATA.*

Page	11	Line	9	For	those	Read	thou
,,	15	,,	13	,,	they	,,	men
,,	18	,,	6	,,	qua	,,	quad
,,	,,	,,	7	,,	drille	,,	rille
,,	,,	,,	11	,,	reluc	,,	reluct
,,	,,	,,	12	,,	tantly	,,	antly
,,	24	,,	22	,,	deaming	,,	dreaming
,,	,,	,,	,,	,,	winged	,,	wing'd
,,	25	,,	12	,,	breath	,,	breadth
,,	30	,,	3	,,	Wardsworth	,,	Wordsworth
,,	31	,,	9	,,	distri	,,	distrib
,,	,;	,,	10	,,	bution	,,	ution
,,	42	,,	13	,,	in	,,	into
,,	49	,,	20	,,	person	,,	persons
,,	56	,,	12	,,	rite	,,	rites
,,	58	,,	3	,,	philanthrophic	,,	philanthropic
,,	64	,,	16	,,	fellow,	,,	fellow

* The haste in which this *brochure* passed through the press has caused so many errors to pass uncorrected for which the writer hopes to be excused.

ERRATA.

Page	Line	For	Read
97	9	bene	Bene
,,	10	institution	Institution
98	25	Causeways	causeways
99	14	censor	censors
,,	,,	cornelious	Cornelius
100	3	speech	words
104	8	£s	£
105	5	honoring	honouring
108	6	The	But

THE
FIRST PARSI BARONET.

CHAPTER I.

Parentage.

At a distance of about 28 miles from the city of Surat, whither the English first came for commerce, lies the village of Nowsaree, a very Paradise in its delightful climate and pure water. Here lived some 100 years since, a worthy couple, conspicuous alike for their good fortune and the noble simplicity of their disposition. They were Chanjeebhoy Wacha and his wife. Chanjeebhoy was active and clever, strong, and of vast worldly experience. Placid in temper, he was gentle at heart and prudent in action; and his wife was not less happily endowed by nature. She was fair in appearance, frank at heart and naturally clever. This pair were, when in their prime of life, blessed with a son, Jeejeebhoy, the father of the subject of this Memoir. When Jejeebhoy arrived at the age of maturity, he was married to one Jeeveebae. The fruit of their happy union was the noble Jamsetjee. He was born on the 15th of July, 1783. From childhood he was smart, and active. He was his father's sole joy. *He* was very happy in him and was always convinced that he would do something great and good, and thereby perpetuate his name. He believed that his son would one day change the circumstances of the family. His mother was equally anxious for the future welfare of her child, and a word from his mouth was sufficient to put her into ecstacies of joy. Thus were the parents proud of their boy, and in thus exciting the admiration and exultation of his parents were the first six years of his life spent. It happened one day about this time that Jamsetjee and his mother went out for a walk in a garden close by. As they were enjoying the delightful appearance of the green foliage and the cool and balmy air, a sudden fit of gloominess overtook Jeeveebae's face and she began to slacken her pace. Sorrow took the place of joy in her heart and tears of regret began to flow from her eyes. The boy was alarmed at this sight. He asked her the cause of these unexpected sorrow and tears. To which inquiry she replied in the following strain.

"My dear son, since yester-night my mind has presented some strange portent. I feel nervous, and my heart tells me that I am soon to leave my friends and family; to forsake this worldly pomp and make my abode in the blessed regions above. This has shot an arrow of disappointment into my bosom, and I am unable to see who shall now take care of thee, oh noble son! In thee I was always proud, and I thought that no mother could produce the like of thee. I had fondly imagined that I should see thee surrounded by pomp and pride, but my hopes are about to be frustrated by the victories of the grave. It is pity to find that we shall soon be apart from each other. Who will be thy mother now? Who will take thee in her arms and kiss and caress thee? In thee my hopes were centred, but some power is interfering and depriving me of my hopes. But God's will be done! Fortune's wheel is ever on the move, and it will take us either to the palace or to the cottage." To this the son replied:—

"O mother burden not thy mind with such strange phantasies. Fill not thy heart with doubts and dreadful apprehensions. None know the decrees of Providence. Observe patience, do not give way to sorrow, but pray to God and he will help thee. For my part, so long as blood flows in my veins I will not allow a particle of gloom to enter thy bosom." These gentle words pierced her heart, and it could not contain itself for joy, but found vent in the exclamation, "Oh dear son, I am conscious of thy good qualities, and I am perfectly certain thou wilt never give me any cause for grief. But alas! my dream appears to me but too true; so be thou prepared for the occasion. I know thou wilt do thy best for me, but man's actions are subservient to the will of God and if he wishes that I should enter his palace, all thy endeavours to keep me here will be as naught. So dear, when Fate decrees that I should leave thee, be not disappointed for a moment. God is great and when I leave thee, the earth below will be thy mother and guardian." When these words were heard by him, his face grew pale and though dreading the occasion, he was inwardly prepared for the sad catastrophe.

CHAPTER II.

The years of childhood glided by, and with the advance of years Jamsetjee made rapid strides in mental and moral progress. All went smoothly till he arrived at his 13th year, when suddenly the worst of predictions was fulfilled. One still evening as the happy couple with their darling child were sitting and conversing together, an intruder entered their presence. He had neither body nor soul, he was a phantom. Jeeveebae saw him, and being preinformed of his visit, stood up at once and received the sad visitor. All was still: the father and child were looking at each other, meanwhile the phantom passed away with the spirit of Jeeveebae. Full of hopes it went away, leaving the body to crumble into dust. Sad days passed with the father and child, but sadder still awaited the latter. Ere six months had run their round, Jamsetjee was an orphan. The death of his wife was a severe blow to Jeejeebhai, and from the day of her death he began to decline in health. For five months did he linger thus, but at last he felt the hand of death on him. When on the verge of eternity he called his son to his bedside, and thus spoke to him.

"Though thou art young in years thou art old in wisdom. Hear then my words and be on thy guard. This world is a false one and it will never come to thine assistance. It is ever changing and careless. When thou art poverty-stricken, it will ever stand aloof from thee. Nor aught of Virtue will it teach, thee; but will take thee to the path of Vice. Yet as the sun, although enveloped in clouds, at last comes out in all his brilliancy, so does a man of good qualities avoid the syren Vice and walk in Virtue's way. Sow not the seeds of that tree to-day, which tomorrow may injure thee in its fruits. He is not a wise man, who trusts his body to the fangs of a serpent, for naught but poison is the result of the deed. So is that man but imprudent, who abandons himself to the world's pleasures, which ultimately effect his ruin. To thy care I entrust the whole family, so by industry and perseverance prosper thou in thy business, and support them. Be good to all and never fear to do a good action. Bring about the ruin of none, nor hurt even an insect. Take delight in relieving the poor, and always lend a helping hand to those who are in need."

With these words he ended and taking his son's hand he sang thus:—

> Father of all, to thee I come,
> My sins forgive, if there be some;
> To thy kind care I leave my son,
> For Parents, Guardians he has none:
> O make him great, oh make him sage!
> Assist him now in orphanage;
> Thy choicest gifts upon him pour,
> Of blessings let him have in store;
> Proclaim his name both far and wide,
> And be his Father, Teacher, Guide!

With these words he gave himself up to his Creator. The caged bird took its way to Heaven, leaving the clay to mingle into dust.

Poor Jamsetjee! He was left alone in the wide world, with no one to care for him, no one to support him! Bereft of parents at an early age he had to make his own way in the world. Such is the portion of all who are so unfortunate as to be deprived of Parents in childhood. Their bold spirits are subdued; their energies depressed, and their activity lulled. What was gaiety and hilarity at first, was now all sorrow and bereavement, and the intrepid spirit of Jamsetjee was by this mournful event, for a time cast down.

CHAPTER III.

But a restless spirit like Jamsetjee's could not long remain passive. After mature consideration he resolved to go to Bombay and there procure a subsistence. On his arrival, he was employed by Mr. Framjee Nusserwanjee Bottlewalla, who afterwards became his father-in-law. This gentleman was then dealing in empty bottles which was at that time a lucrative trade, and he was in a flourishing condition. Here Jamsetjee made some progress both in Gujrati and English in his leisure hours. By his honesty, diligence and integrity he won the confidence of his superior, who now gave the whole concern into his charge. Nor did his love end here. Seeing Jamsetjee every day more zealous in his work and ever trying to do more than he was told to do, he thought of a nearer and a dearer connection with him, than that of the employer and the employed. He had a daughter comely in appearance, fair in features and blessed with

> "Eyes of Fire, lips of dew,
> Cheeks that shame the rose's hue."

Her name was Avabye, the present dowager Lady Jamsetjee Jeejeebhoy. She was a meet bride for the honest Jamsetjee. The match was announced to both parties, and on their agreement, the banns were proclaimed. The guests assembled to honor the occasion, and the priests thus united the happy pair.

"I. May the Creator Ormazd give you many descendants, with men as grand children, much food, friends with heart-ravishing body and countenance, walking through a long life, to the duration of a hundred and fifty years.

2. On the day—————, in the month———

, in the year————, since the king of kings, the ruler Yezdegert, of the stock of Sasan, a congregation is come together in the circle of the fortunate town, Bombay, according to the law and custom of the good Mazdayacnian Law, to give this maiden to a husband; this maiden, this woman, Avabye by name.

3. Do you join with your relations in agreement for this marriage, with honorable mind that pleasure may increase to ye twain?

4. In the name and friendship of Ormazd. Be ever shining, be very enlarged! Be increasing! Be victorious! Learn purity! Be worthy of good praise! May the mind think good thoughts, the words speak good, the works do good! May all wicked thoughts hasten away, all wicked words be diminished, all wicked works be burnt up! Being a Mazdayacnian think and do good. Win for thyself property by right-dealing. Speak truth with the rulers and be obedient. Be modest with friends, clever, and well-wishing. Be not cruel. Be not wrathful-minded. Commit no sin through shame. Be not covetous. Torment not. Cherish not wicked envy, be not haughty, treat no one despitefully, cherish no lust. Rob not the property of others, keep thyself from the wives of others. Do

good works with good activity. Be no companion to a covetous one. Go not on the same way with a cruel one. Enter into no agreement with one of ill fame. Enter not into work in common with an unskilful one. Combat the adversaries with right. Go with friends as is agreeable to friends. Before an assembly speak only pure words. Before kings speak with moderation. From ancestors inherit good names. In no wise displease thy mother. Keep thine own body pure in justice.

5. Be of immortal body, like Kai-khosru. Be understanding, like Kâus. Be shining as the Sun. Be pure as the Moon. Be renowned as Zartusht. Be powerful as Rustom. Be fruitful as the earth. Keep good friendship with friends, brothers, wife and children, as body and soul hold together. Keep always the right faith and good character. Recognise Ormazd as Ruler, Zartusht as lord. Exterminate Ahriman and the Devs.

6. May Ormazd send you gifts, Bahmān, thinking with the soul, Ardibihist good speech, Sharevar good working, Cpendarmat, wisdom, Khardât, sweetness and fatness, Amerdât fruitfulness!

7. May Ormazd bestow gifts on you, the Fire brightness, Ardvicûra purity, the sun exalted rule,

the moon increase, Tir liberality, Gosh abstemiousness, Mithra Fortune, Crosh obedience, Rasn right conduct, Farvardin increase of strength, Behram victory. Ram, might. Arshasvangh enlightenment of wisdom, inheritance of majesty, Astât increase of virtue, Açman great activity, Zamyâd firmness of place, Mahreçpant good heed, Aneran distinction of body.

8. Good art thou, mayst those maintain that which is still better for thee than the good, since thou fittest thyself worthily as a Zaŏta. Mayst thou receive the reward which is earned by the Zaŏta as one who thinks, speaks, and does much good.

9. May that come to you which is better than the good, may that not come to you which is worse than the evil, may that not come to me which is worse than the evil. So may it happen as I pray."

The ceremony here ended. The guests repaired to the saloon where a rich repast was laid out. The night passed in gaiety and pleasure, and in singing,

"Let a set of sober asses
Rail against the joys of drinking,
While water, tea,
And milk agree,
To set cold brains a thinking.
Power and wealth,
Beauty, health,

> Wit and mirth in wine are crowned;
> Joys abound,
> Pleasure's found,
> Only where the *glass* goes round."

CHAPTER IV.

HERE ends the boyhood of Jamsetjee, and now he enters upon a career of life which ultimately makes his name famous throughout the world. And here by the way we may mention a story that passes current among us, and proves that although wealth greatly assisted him in his benevolence, he was naturally of a charitable disposition. It is said that every morning as he was going to his office in the Fort, be used to give to the poor that sat on the Esplanade a pie each, thereby spending every day two annas worth of pies:—a practice which he kept up and extended as his means increased till the close of his life. This story must at once silence the scandal-tipped tongues of those who aver that his sole motives in being charitable were vanity and ostentation.

But to resume. The time had now come when Jamsetjee thought that he must direct his mind to far higher aims than those of a mere manager-ship of a bottleshop. He thought of enlarging his ideas of the world and its commerce by visiting different countries. With this view he joined his cousin Mr. Merwanjee Maneckjee Tuback in a voyage to China, going with him in the capacity of clerk in the year 1799. He was then about sixteen years of age. Mr. Merwanjee was a wellknown merchant both in Bombay and China, and under him Jamsetjee was thoroughly grounded in the principles and details of commerce. By a diligent discharge of his duties he satisfied his superior, and they returned to Bombay each with a favourable opinion of the other. Taking advantage of the experience thus obtained and wishing to venture a little on his own account, Jamsetjee became a partner with his father-in-law, and went to China again there to pay his devotions at the shrine of Fortune. It is said that when he went on his first voyage with his cousin Mr. Merwanjee Tuback, his private property amounted to no more than a hundred and thirty Rupees, and that when he returned to these shores he had not increased his fortune by more than fifty Rupees in a year and a half of service;—an unequivocal proof of the rigid honesty with which he must have served his superior. But virtue brings its own reward, and when he went on this his second voyage many had so great a confidence in his honesty and integrity that they readily lent him, a poor man, the large sum of thirtyfive thousand Rupees to commence with.

"Who comprehends his trust and to the same
Keeps faithful with a singleness of aim;
And therefore does not stoop, nor lie in wait
For wealth, of honour, or for worldly state;
Whom they must follow, on whose head must fall,
Like showers of manna, if they come at all"

Their con-fidence was not abused, and no sooner was he in a position to do so, then he returned every pie of the money he had borrowed, interest and all, and humbly rested thankful for the favour. His character as a merchant was now every day increasing, and Rupees began plentifully to flow into his coffers. But the money was hard-earned. In his second voyage to China his ship was overtaken by storm, just as she was on the point of entering the harbour, and with great discomfort he escaped the impending disaster. Nor was his return to Bombay the less fraught with fear. Before the ship had proceeded half-way, the enemies of the English were seen menacing at a distance. But here we must digress a little from our subject.

At this period of the world's history, the famous French Revolution of 1789 was at its height. Ten dreadful years had now passed since its first outbreak and yet was it not crushed. It was a period of violence, tumult and destruction; a period throughout which, as Creasy remarks, "the wealth of nations was scattered like sand, and the blood of nations lavished like water"; in short it was a dark and dreadful epoch unparalleled in the annals of history. The wars had spread blood and desolation from Cadiz to Moscow, and from Naples to Copenhagen; they had wasted the means of human enjoyment, and destroyed the instruments of social improvement. Nor was the contest confined to Europe only, but it had made its appearance even in India, where like hungry lions they were lying in ambush to pounce upon their first victim. Neither sea nor earth had any respite from the dissolute and ferocious habits of a predatory soldiery, and everywhere the cry was "The Foe, They come! Thy come!" The sacred rights of commerce were even discarded, and every merchant ship was as welcome a prey as a man-of-war. Hence every merchantship was then accompanied by a man-of-war to guard against the possibility of the enemies lighting upon it and depriving it of its cargo.

In one of these ships Jamsetjee had taken a passage for Bombay. As stated before, ere the ship had compassed half its journey, a French man-of-war was seen in the distance hoisting its colours. The English ship was commanded by a brave admiral Sir Nathaniel Dance, a perfect English gentleman, and so used to war that he could withstand its shock. The French were under the guidance of M. Loinois, a very courageous man who had taken to war from his infancy. Both Commanders had been longing for war, each conscious of

> "The stern joy that warriors feel,
> In foemen worthy of their steel,"

and rejoicing in the opportunity. The French were the offensive party, and they rather took the English by surprise. Obliged to make the best of the opportunity, Sir Nathaniel at once prepared for defence. He took up the telescope and measured the strength of the foe. They had summoned up their blood and lent their eyes a terrible aspect. His own men were no less burning with revenge. While shone the sun he made his hay.) In their enthusiasm he ordered his men to fire. The French ships began to give way near the balls of the English, and amidst the noise of the cannons and the shrieks of his men, M. Loinois was at a loss what to do. Thinking discretion to be the better part of valour, he took to his heels. Away went the French fleet in "confusion worse confounded"

AFTER THE BATTLE.

and on went the English to pursue them to the last. The sea was red with blood; the sky obscured by smoke; the French were filled with dismay, the English with joy. Aloud they spoke, " Hurra! the foes are moving!" and with hearts full of mercy they allowed the enemy to go unmolested. The gentle sex who had fainted away now began to revive, and with their fair appearance shed a ray of glory on the scene. The poop of battle was converted into a music hall, and the gentlemen joined the ladies in a dance. "Fast goes the fiddle, merrily twirl their feet, loudly rattles the jovial laughter, while thus they enjoy their fun.

> "Away they go,
> Heel and toe,
> Some on one leg,
> Some on two.

Faster plays the fiddle, not to be outdone, faster they go—twirl faster, faster still—amid shouts of laughter and approving plaudits, till at last a sudden wave makes the vessel give a terrific roll, and away the dancers go into the scuppers, where they lie laughing or scrambling, or helplessly contemplating the quiet grave face of the moon." "And so cheerily goes the ship, while the wind blows fair"!

This was a wonderful sight to Jamsetjee! awe struck first by the appearance of the enemy, his cup of joy was now filled to the brim. The nimble-footed step of the English lady was a marked contrast to the awkward movements of the Indian dancing girl. The polka, the waltz, the quadrille, and the other merry-going tunes of the English delighted him so much that he forgot his native *Gajals* and *Thoomries*. He was now as it were in a paradise; and when the brave flag was seen gaily flowing on Fort St. George, he reluctantly left the " wooden walls " of " auld England " for " the towers of proud Bombay."

CHAPTER V.

Jamsetjee's landing on the Apollo Pier was a signal of joy to his family. He came as a respectable merchant now and extended his transactions not only to the celestial city, but to Bengal, Madras, the west coast of Sumatra, Singapore, Siam, the Archipelago, Alexandria, and England. Nor was he yet satisfied with his accumulations. Avarice entrapped him in her snare and he fell a victim to her. As if the hardships he had suffered in his late voyage were insufficient to test his powers of facing danger, he went to sea again on his fifth and last voyage to China. He was now in his twentyfourth year, and after remaining in China for about a year, and gathering the fruits of a plentiful commercial harvest, he thought of returning to Bombay, there to spend his money in unostentatious charity, and in ameliorating the condition of his poor countrymen. And as if to teach him what the miseries of the poor are, and how to improve them, the Almighty Creator now placed him in a position which has rendered the career of his life half-heroic. As he was returning from China his ship was captured by the French. Unlike the former occasion the French now greatly exceeded the English in number. It would have been rashness to attempt any resistance, and as the enemy spared them their lives, the English had no other resource than quietly to capitulate. This done, the French took possession of their cargo and fleet, took the passengers in their own vessel, and treated them humanely, till they reached the Cape of Good Hope where they were landed.

Unhappy Jamsetjee! he had lost all his rich cargo, and was left without a single pie and without a single dress, except the one he had on his body at the time. He was half dead with hunger and thirst when he placed his foot on the Dutch shore, for the Cape of Good Hope was then a neutral town in the hands of the Dutch. Knight describes the general character of the country as sterile and uninviting. Some part of it, as for instance the environs of Cape Town are indeed picturesque, but on the whole "the characteristics of the scenery are rocky and arid mountains, naked uncultivated plains, stony valleys without a tree, a prevailing monotony, and absence of shade, of verdure and of water." Who would not pity the plight of Jamsetjee at this time? From a merchant rolling in riches, he was turned adrift on a land with whose language he was unacquainted, and where he knew not a soul, to walk barefooted, in tattered clothes, gaining a scanty and precarious subsistence from the charitable dole of strangers, and grown gaunt and wretched from the hardships of unaccustomed privations! Justly did he curse the day and the star that enticed him away from his "home, sweet home," to gather hoards of which, he now thought, he could make no use.

Well may his sufferings be compared to those of Job. Through the machinations of Satan, Job lost his cattle, his children, was forsaken by friends, and afflicted with dire diseases. By the seizure of the French, Jamsetjee lost all his rich cargo, his children were to all purposes dead to him, and being destitute of shelter, he was shivering with the bitter cold by night and burning with the heat of the sun by day. Yet like Job he suffered all this quietly till exhausted, he sought relief in a flow of tears. For he thought,

> "Though losses and crosses
> Be lessons right severe,
> There's wit there, you'll get there,
> You'll find no other where."

Evil times however soon pass by. One morning, as he was sitting alone on the steps of a house, he heard that some ladies and gentlemen were to leave the place for Calcutta in a Dutch ship. With heart full of joy he rose up, and after a few words of prayer, he straightway went in search of the party who were about to go. He found them, and told them how rich he had been, how he had been brought to that place, how much he had suffered while there, and implored them to take pity on him and allow him to proceed with them to Calcutta, whence he could go to his native country, and there remember this act of charity so long as memory itself existed. Words like these soon excited the quality of mercy in the breasts of the fair, ones, and one of them comforted the unhappy youth with reassuring words; giving him at the same time much good advice, and promising to assist him to the utmost of her power, saying in conclusion,

> "If what shone afar so grand,
> Turn to nothing in thy hand,
> On again, the virtue lies
> In the struggle, not the prize."

These words brought tears into the eyes of Jamsetjee, and his heart became so full of gratitude, that he was unable to utter a word. He thanked the gentle lady for her advice, and promising to keep it always engraved in his heart, he shook hands with all the party, and went his way.

Immediately after his departure the truly generous lady repaired to the English consul. She acquainted him with Jamsetjee's miserable plight and asked his assistance. He tendered it without a moment's delay, sent for Jamsetjee, and gave him clean clothes, a hearty repast, and a present of twenty dollars. With the music of his sweet words he soothed the grieved soul of Jamsetjee. He was sent on board the steamer with the ladies. The fresh balmy air of the sea enlivened him again. His drooping spirit once more held its head on high, and his tottering feet once more regained their native strength. The voyage was comfortable in the extreme, and beguiling the time with music and dancing, they arrived safely in Calcutta. On landing, Jamsetjee offered his prayers to God, and reflected with a sense of heartfelt gratitude that he was once more in the land of freedom and safety. He stopped in Calcutta about four weeks to regain his lost strength as well as to observe the commercial capabilities of that part of the world. As the lion is always in search of his prey, the warrior in search of glory, so the merchant keeps his eyes ever and anon bent upon commercial enterprize. The diamond sparkles even in the dust, the sun is apparent even in a cloudy sky, even so the really intelligent man will shine out in all his radiance, although enveloped in the mist of darkness. So is the

"Active doer, noble liver,
Strong to labour, sure to conquer."

CHAPTER VI.

Hence Jamsetjee now set out for, what Dave Carson calls, " our tight little, cramped little island." On his arrival at home the friends gathered together to hear his tale " of wondrous beauty." They had all given him up ; so his arrival set their troubled hearts at rest. As they heard his tale of sorrow and privation, they wondered more and more at his marvellous powers of endurance, and thanked heaven that it had restored him to them. To him came now the lovely Avabye with eyes sparkling with bright hopes and face beaming with the signs of joy. They rushed into each others' arms and tears of joy marked the embrace. She, to whom was, as Dryden says,

> "His life the theme of her eternal prayer,
> Tis scarce so much his guardian angel's care!
> Not summer morns such mildness can disclose,
> The Hermon lily, nor the Sharon rose."

then opened her lips and said, "Heaven be praised that it has restored thee to my bosom! May the Almighty Creator be as ever merciful to thee! Each day and night wore heavily on me, and my bed has been one of thorns in thy absence. Why art thou so pale and sickly? Why is thy speech so faltering? Who made thee so miserable? Oh tell me, tell me that, dear."

> "Oh! many a night on this lone couch reclined,
> My deaming fear with storms hath winged the wind,
> And deemed the breath that faintly fanned thy sail.
> The murmuring prelude of the ruder gale;
> Though soft, it seemed the low prophetic dirge,
> That mourned thee floating on the savage surge.
> Still would I rise to rouse the beacon fire,
> Lest spies less true should let the blaze expire;

And many a restless hour outwatched each star,
And morning came—and still thou wert afar.
Oh! how the chill blast on my bosom blew,
And day broke dreary on my troubled view,
And still I gazed and gazed—and not a prow
Was granted to my tears—my truth—my vow!
At length—'t was noon—I hailed and blest the mast
That met my sight—it neared—Alas! it past!
Another came—Oh God! 'twas thine at last!"

On these words, he looked her fully in the face, and cried with joy. He told her of "his hairbreath escape in the imminent deadly breach," of "his being taken by the insolent foe," and so forth, and then as it were cried with Othello,

"O my soul's joy,
If after every tempest come such calms,
May the winds blow till they have waken'd death,
And may the labouring bark climb hills of seas
Olympus high, and duck again as low as hell's,
from heaven!
If it were now to die,' twere now to be most happy,
For I fear, my soul hath her content so absolute,
That not another comfort like to this succeeds in unknown fate"

To which Avabye replied Desdemonalike,

"The Heavens forbid, but that our loves and comforts
Should increase even as our days do grow"

From this time, 1807, Jamsetjee never left his country, but remained all his life in Bombay. With redoubled zeal and industry, he extended his commercial relations, directing all his affairs by the light of that discerning calculation which always stood him in such good stead. He always availed himself of the best opportunity, for as the Latin poet says " opportunity has hair in front, behind she is bald; if you seize her by the forelock you may hold her, but if suffered to escape, not Jupiter himself can catch her again." He tried his fortune in every direction, and <u>fortune smiled serenely upon</u> him on every side. Neither Bengal, nor Madras, nor China, nor Singapore, nor Siam, nor even the mighty realm of our virtuous Queen, could help acknowledging the superiority of his mercantile tactics; and poured cash into his coffers. His credit was now unbounded, and aided by *mens conscia recti* and a kind Deity he tried on every side and won the day.

> "Fame, like a light, shone broadening on before
> His path, and cleaved the shadows on the ground;
> High deeds and gentle, bruited near and far,
> Show where that soul went flashing as a star."

Through him the name of the Parsis resounded throughout the civilized world. By his rapid manœuvres he surprised the oldest and most experienced merchants of the day, and when they receded from the field, he boldly came forward and gained the palm. The market, fluctuating as it was, was in his hands, and it was in his power to mould it to his purpose. Like our sharp Hindoo friend, Mr. Premchund Roychund, who had lately the control of the sharemarket, he could make lacs in cotton and opium in a day. He was the boldest speculator of the period, and truly speaking speculation seemed to have reached its climax in his time. But he speculated in broad daylight, and used no mean artifices and backstair influence to rig the market. Taking advantage of the war that was raging in Europe at the time, and anticipating a rise in the price of cotton, he shipped thousands of bales, and got what others were afraid to risk. " Nothing venture, nothing win;" " hazard all, and gain all." He hazarded his all and gained all that he could get by honest means. English, Parsis, and Hindoos bowed to his genius, and confessed his superiority in mercantile affairs. He had a good deal of connection with the firms of Messrs. Remington and Co. and Messrs. Jardine, Matheson and Co., a connection which more or less exists up to the present time. Mr. Jardine was a gentleman of moderate means at first, and it is solely through the agency he carried on of Jamsetjee's affairs, that his House is now in a flourishing and healthy condition in China. Nor were Jamsetjee's agents alone benefited by his ventures. His muccadums and servants are now well off. He had, in his concern, three junior partners:—men who were the types of honesty and integrity. Each of them belonged to a different race. The first was a Hindoo by name, Motichund Amichund, the very essence of a "mild Hindoo." The second was a Parsi, one Furdoonjee Sorabjee Paruck, the worthy father of a noble son, Sett Cursetjee Furdoonjee Paruck, who has made his name a synonym for unostentatious charity and liberality in Bombay and Gujrat. The third was a Concanese Mussulman, by name Mahomed Rogay, who was a very pious and good-natured man.

With partners of good qualities like these, Jamsetjee carried on his business unremittingly from his arrival in Bombay in 1807 to the year from whence the stream of his charity began to flow, 1822. In these fifteen years, he amassed a colossal fortune, estimated at about two crores of Rupees. Well might he then exclaim with Sir Humphrey Davy, "What I am I have made myself: I say this without vanity, and in pure simplicity of heart."

He who works earnestly, energetically and with

purpose seldom meets with failure. The poet says,

> "Rich are the diligent, who can command
> Time, nature's stock! and could his hourglass fall,
> Would, as for seed of stars stoop for the sand,
> And, by incessant labour, gather all."

and he is perfectly correct, for he who falls a prey to idleness will ever be unfortunate, but he who works hard is sure to be supplied with plenty. Men do not gather grapes from thorns, or figs from thistles. It is the bitter pill that makes us healthy. The portion of a coward is misfortune and shame. Grasp a nettle boldly and its sting is unfelt. It was courage, industry, hardship and fortitude that made Jamsetjee what he became. He obeyed to a letter the poet's advice, who said,

> "See first that the design is wise and just;
> That ascertained, pursue it resolutely.
> Do not for one repulse forego the purpose
> That you resolved to effect."

In his childhood he was steeped in poverty and from poverty he rose to greatness. And when that pinnacle was once attained, he spent the remainder of his life in deeds of active benevolence and usefulness to his fellow men. When the farmer poet of Scotland speaks of money that it is

> "Not for to hide it in a hedge,
> Nor for a train attendant,
> But for the glorious privilege
> Of being independent."

he alludes to the sturdy independence of the Scotchmen and their neighbours, of which they are so proud. And justly too; for although Wardsworth says that dependence and independence must go together, men would rather have the latter alone than associated with the former. And when that manly independence is once obtained, and there be left something with us that is superfluous, it is the duty of all to distribute that superfluity among their less fortunate fellow-creatures, exhorting them to follow their examples, and use the little they may get to advantage. And if possible we would advise all who may be bestowing gifts on their inferiors, to act as the lord in the New Testament did with his servants, ask from them an account of the way in which they made use of the gifts; and if to advantage, to double their portion in future. Jamsetjee nearly approached this standard—He made a good use of the little he got from others and improved it manifold. He became independent and withal rich enough to make others so. He placed all sorts of facilities in the way of his inferiors, and with tenderness and love eyed their prospects. Gentle reader, this is true charity. If thou hast means, do the same. Peruse with care an account of the good deeds that Jamsetjee has done with a judicious liberality, and make a name that shall to future ages "point a moral or adorn a tale." For of the good men who have left us, the poet says,

> "Ever their phantoms rise before us,
> Our loftier brothers, but one in blood;
> By bed and table they lord it o'er us,
> With looks of beauty and with words of good."

CHAPTER VII.

Jamsetjee's hour of trouble had now passed away and that of a quiet enjoyment and generous distribution of wealth begun. In the year of grace, 1822, he came forward for the first time as an alleviator of the miseries of his countrymen. His first act of charity was the payment of the debts of as many men as were then in the civil gaol. This cost him the sum of Rupees three thousand.

In 1824 an event took place which once more opened the coffers of Jamsetjee. The disastrous ravages of fire destroyed an Agiary or fire-temple of the Parsees in Surat. Being too poor to rebuild the temple, the Suratees applied to Jamsetjee for aid. It was no sooner asked than given, for he devoted a sum of fifteen thousand Rupees to this pious work, which remains a lasting monument of his piety and generosity.

Ere four years had run their round, Bombay, Poona and Gujrat witnessed another of Jamsetjee's noble benefactions. To perform the religious ceremonies of the Ghambars,* and to give a feast on those days to all the Zoroastrians of these places, he gave a lac and seventy-five thousand Rupees towards their Fund. It was given into the hands of five trustees, Mr. James Henry Crawford, Messrs. Remington &Co., Sett Cursetjee Jamsetjee (the present noble Baronet) and Setts Furdoonjee Sorabjee Paruck and Mahomed Rogay. Copies of the trust-deed which was signed in 1838, are now deposited with the firms of Messrs. Remington &Co. of Bombay, Messrs Colvin and Sleechovy of Calcutta, and in Jamsetjee's own firm. This benefaction is one of the most pious that a Zoroastrian could perform.

The devouring element once more played mischief in Surat in 1837. Its ravages were the most dreadful that could be pictured to our mind's eye. Like the fire of London, it destroyed streets after streets, and its force was unchecked for twelve consecutive days. It subsided at last, but not without exercising its disastrous influence on the status of

---

*Religious festivals among the Parsis, occurring six times annually, and lasting for five consecutive days.

society. Men of position and standing were levelled with the poor, whilst the latter were without shelter, food, or clothing. Twenty thousand houses were burnt to the ground. In this exigency the benevolent Jamsetjee came forward with a ready hand, and at once sent a sum of thirty-five thousand Rupees to Surat, together with some bags of rice. The poor were fed and clothed. No distinction was made of caste or creed in this good act, a fact reflecting on him the greatest credit. The occasion has now passed away, but the glory of the act will resound throughout the world.

About seven miles from Bombay is a place called Mahim. Between it and Bandora there was no passage by land, and travellers were reduced to the painful necessity of crossing in a common native boat which used to be every now and then upset and cost many a life. Many attempts were made to prevent this but in vain. In 1837, Government sent Captain Foster to survey the place, and to estimate the cost of a causeway between Mahim and Bandora. It was estimated at sixty-seven thousand Rupees. On this Sett. Cursetjee Cowasjee Banajee wrote to Government, and asked them to contribute to the work a sum of ten thousand Rupees, as well as to use the ten thousand

Rupees in this undertaking which were subscribed by the native gentlemen of Bombay for the construction of the Tanna Causeway. The balance of the sum required he offered to collect by subscription. On Government complying with this proposition, Mr. Cursetjee set about collecting subscriptions, but, alas! to no effect. The work was thus deferred till 1841, when Mr. Cursetjee met Jamsetjee, and on the former's touching on the subject of the Causeway, Jamsetjee at once promised that he would defray the whole of the expense towards its construction. With this view, he wrote a letter to Government on the 23rd of February 1841, and generously offered to construct the Causeway. Mr. Morris who was at that time Chief Secretary to Government, conveyed to Jamsetjee in a letter dated the 21st May, 1842, the thanks of Government, and enclosed the plan of Mr. Crawford, the engineer, with its rough estimate amounting to one lac, sixty four thousand five hundred and forty Rupees: a sum nearly three times as great as the former. Jamsetjee considered this too much, and so in a letter, dated the 31st of August, 1842, he wrote to Government to invite, through the Military Board, tenders for the work. This was accordingly done, and the tender of Mr. Jamsetjee Dorabjee, our well-known Railway contractor, for Rupees one lac thirtysix thousand, seven hundred and eighty, was accepted and sent to Jamsetjee by the Chief Secretary, Mr. Pringle, on the 19th December, 1842. Jamsetjee agreed to this arrangement, and with his letter of the 19th of January, 1843, he enclosed a cheque for one lac of Rupees, and after a few months gave a further sum of fifteen thousand Rupees. And now the good work was begun and by the close of 1845, it was finished. "It consists of a huge mound of loose stones above 2000 feet or considerably upwards of half a mile in length. It varies from ten to twentyfour feet in height from the roadway to the bottom, and reaches to the height of five feet above high water. It is thirty-two feet across the top, and from forty to seventy at bottom, varying with the depth. The carriage way is twenty feet broad, with a foot-path four and a half feet on each side. The parapet walls are three feet high, on the sea side two feet thick, and on the land side eighteen inches. For about two thirds of the line across the channel it varies from ten to eighteen feet in depth; the remaining third is filled up with hard trap rock to nearly high water mark. By a bold stroke of engineering, the main channel has been entirely built across with a solid mound of stone so as to prevent either ingress or egress to the waters beyond a certain depth. On the rocky portion a bridge of one hundred and fiftyeight feet in length, consisting of four elliptical arches, of thirty feet span each, is set down. Through this the surface water is compelled to find its way, and it rushes through accordingly at the rate of six or seven miles an hour. The noise of the current is heard at full a mile off." The work has been done by a masterly hand, and is an excellent monument of the triumph of Art over Nature. On the fourth of April 1846, the Causeway was opened with great éclat. "An immense concourse of every race and kindred, shade and line, had assembled at an early hour in the afternoon to witness the spectacle. The road from Byculla to Mahim Wood presented an almost continuous line of vehicles from the bullock hackery to the Long Acre chariot. Four six pounder guns under the command of Captain Unwin, a party of Lancers with detachments of the 2nd Queen's Royals and Native Infantry with their bands, the Governor's band, together with a very strong body of horse and foot police, were at the ground a little after three o'clock. At five precisely the Governor and Staff arrived, and the procession having been marshalled in the following order, as previously intimated at a given signal, moved along towards the entrance of the Causeway, on nearing the middle of which the cannon thundered forth a royal salute :

    The Engineer Officer who constructed the Causeway.
                      His Establishment.
                     An Escort of Lancers.
          The Hon'ble the Governor's Band.
    Gentlemen on horseback on either side of the carriages.

The procession was closed by an Escort of Lancers.

An elegant triumphal arch had been erected across the Causeway at the Mahim and another on the Salsette end, and beyond this latter, under the great banian trees, was a splendid marquee, whither the company repaired for refreshment. Lines of flags and pennons had been placed along both sides of the roadway, on the summits of the triumphal arches, and at both extremities of the Velard. A splendid collation, with every rarity that culinary art could supply, was arranged in the marquee. The ladies of the Jamsetjee family were waited on by the Governor, the Commander-in-chief, Lady MacMohun, Mr. and Mrs. Reid, Mr. and Mrs. Willoughby, and other distinguished guests. The party remained here for about an hour, the bands playing outside. The party having assembled round the table, the Hon'ble the Governor spoke as follows :—

Sir Jamsetjee Jeejeebhoy—This is an occasion which affords me the highest gratification, and I would wish to preface my remarks with a few general observations. Some years back it was suggested to the Government the desirableness of erecting a causeway between Mahim and Bandora, but owing to the state of its finances, the improvement was abandoned, and for the present the matter fell to the ground. Some three or four years back the then Government caused a survey to be made and the estimate of the Engineer was prepared and presented, but owing to a demand on its resources from other quarters, they were compelled to postpone the consideration of the subject. In the year 1841, two very great calamities occurred, viz, the upsetting of from fifteen to twenty boats while attempting during the monsoon to cross the river, occasioning a great loss of life. Lady Jamsetjee, on hearing of these dreadful accidents enquired, why do not the Government build a bridge across these waters to prevent such accidents? and on hearing that for the present the rulers of the land were not prepared to carry out such projects as

LADY JAMSETJEE'S PROPOSAL.

would prevent a recurrence of them stated that she herself, out of her private fortune, would willingly defray the expense, were she made acquainted with the actual outlay required. Upon this an Estimate was framed which like the estimates of Engineer officers generally was in the end found to be a very long way behind the actual cost. The estimate presented at that period computed that 67,000 Rupees were sufficient to complete the undertaking, but after this sum had been expended, it was found that it was in comparison scarcely òne third of what was absolutely needed. Lady Jamsetjee then, rather than that the work should stop, increased her donation to a lac of Rupees, and on it being intimated to her that even this sum was insufficient to defray the expenses of items of outlay which had not been included in the estimate, contributed a further sum of 10,000 Rupees, shortly after her previous contribution. The Court of Directors were then applied to by the existing Government, but Lady Jamsetjee, fearing delay in such an application, further added to her former subscriptions the several sums of four, six, and ten thousand rupees, making a total gift to this most useful and most important undertaking, of the sum of (1,40,000) one lac and forty thousand Rupees. The reply of the Court of Directors, with the usual liberality for which they are famed, more particularly in any object tending to promote the welfare and prosperity of the Natives of this country, acceded to the request that all further expense should be defrayed by them, and the work went on advancing rapidly towards completion. Only the day before yesterday I heard that a handsome approach was suggested to the Causeway, and that the want of further funds prohibited its being carried into execution. I have since been informed that on this circumstance reaching the ears of Lady Jamsetjee, she, with her usual unbounded liberality, immediately consented to defray the expense, estimated at Rupees (22,000) twenty-two thousand in addition to a former five thousand required for the embankment, &c; thus a grand total of the donations of this most liberal and generous Lady, amounting for this useful undertaking alone to the sum of one lac and sixty seven thousand Rupees. Lady Jamsetjee had frequently urged that, as the poorer classes of the community were concerned, it was no more than right and just that the rich should contribute to their wants. In thus noticing the liberality of her Ladyship, I cannot but avail myself of the opportunity of mentioning circumstances which to some here present may be totally unknown. I allude, Sir Jamsetjee, to the very great liberality of your family. From a memorandum that I made some two years back, and from what I have since been able to collect, though many of your deeds of charity are hidden from the sight of all men, I sum up, that no less a sum than (100,000 £) one hundred thousand pounds sterling, has been subscribed by your family for Public Works: and when I come to place this sum in juxtaposition with the gifts of British Merchants, I say, give me a Bombay Merchant. It matters not to what creed they may belong, as they are created of one and the same God;—and the act of benevolence and charity will, it is to be hoped, have its weight eventually. I shall now conclude by proposing "The health of Lady Jamsetjee"; and that she and Sir Jamsetjee and family, may for many years be blessed with health and prosperity."

The toast was responded to with three cheers and one cheer more, where-upon Jamsetjee in a modest speech thanked His Excellency the Governor on behalf of his wife, and said that in doing the deeds that His Excellency had been good enough to take notice of, he had done nothing but his duty towards God and Man.

The assembly then separated, and all hearts were pleased to see a work which has since saved many lives which used annually to fall victims to Neptune's wrath.

As if not to be behindhand in supplying the other element that is necessary to human nature, viz, water, Jamsetjee now undertook a work which will for ever bear testimony to his truly charitable disposition. The Capital of the Deccan, the seat of the Mahrattas, was destitute of a sufficient supply of pure water. The ingenious Hindoo in the dynasty of the Mahrattas had by his engineering skill directed the waters of the rivers Mutta and Mulla, which empty themselves in the Bay of Bengal, but take their rise in the towering Ghauts that are the natural bulwarks of Poona, so as to drive them to the place of habitation. But on the passing of Poona from the hands of the Mahrattas to those of the English, the work was left neglected and uncared for. When however, it became the head quarters of the army of the Bombay Presidency, their eyes were opened, but as the expenses attending the rebuilding of the work were great, the Government hesitated to sanction the outlay. The inhabitants of the eastern part of the town were also suffering from the scarcity of water. At this juncture, the ready purse of Jamsetjee came to their rescue. In a letter dated the 5th of February 1844, he expressed his desire to Government to rebuild the works. They readily acceded to his wishes, in a letter dated the 8th idem, and the work was at once begun. Two Mahrattas named Venkatesh Narayen and Heera Ramchundra, undertook to build the Bund, as it is called, for Rupees seventy-three thousand nine hundred and forty five, and the machinery and engineers to set it up were ordered from England by Jamsetjee through Messrs. Forbes & Co. The work was completed in 1845, but the *chunam* work being *cucha*, it was swept away by the swollen tides of the Mutta and Mulla. It was once more ready by 1847, when a similar calamity again befel it, but the third attempt was successful. The machinery being now put up, it was in working order by the end of 1848. This is a work to which too much praise cannot be assigned. To appreciate its advantages it needs but to be seen. The large sum of one lac, seventeen thousand four hundred and eighty one Rupees was spent on this very important work.

This was a work of universal importance to the people of Poona. But an undertaking, for the sole benefit of his caste-fellows there, was in the hands of Jamsetjee. On a request being preferred by them, he built for them an Agiary or Firetemple in 1841, at a cost of forty-five thousand Rupees. He also laid aside for its repairs Rupees ten thousand, and entrusted them to the hands of worthy men. He exhorted his countrymen there to join in the pious work, and requested them to look after it with great care.

But now he surprised the people of Bombay with another benevolent act. On the 20th of February 1839, he called a meeting of the Parsis there. When all had arrived; Jamsetjee rose up and with modest humility approached the venerable Sett Nowrojee Wadia, and handed over to him two documents. One was the deed of gift of a place which he had bought out of the Fort of Bombay, and where he had built an extensive building at a cost of seventy thousand Rupees. The second was a similar deed of three large shops he had near Chinch Bunder. He gave the first place for the free use of the Parsis on all occasions, and out of the rent of the latter, the expenses of the former were to be defrayed for ever. The assembled multitude were agreeably surprised by this noble benefaction, and Sett Nowrojee Wadia returned thanks on behalf of the meeting to Jamsetjee.

Once more the Deccan attracted Jamsetjee's

THE DHARAMSALA AT KHANDALLA. 45

ready sympathy. Half way between Bombay and Poona is the plateau of Khandalla. It is a delightful little place, and at all seasons of the year the climate is favourable to health. In the rains especially the station looks one beautiful garden of fruits and flowers, and the aspect is rendered more enchanting by the presence of a marked contrast between the imposing appearance of the stately Ghauts around and the dreadful and awe-inspiring sights of the valleys below. At this time of the year, Jamsetjee went there. One fine morning as he was standing at his window, and enjoying the pleasant and agreeable sight, he saw some poor travellers standing out, wet from top to toe, and unable to find a shelter. Jamsetjee was much grieved at this sight, and thinking the miseries of such people had a claim upon his benevolence, he at once made up his mind of building a Dharamsala for the poor of every caste and creed. He came to Bombay, and taking with him Setts Jeejeebhoy Dadabhoy, Cursetjee Rustomjee Wadia, Vicajee Mherjee, and Mahomed Rogay, he went back to Khandalla to select the proper site for his undertaking. This being done, the work was at once begun. The cost of the building is estimated at twenty thousand Rupees.

The building is an inestimable boon to travellers by rail between Bombay and Poona.

But "fair Bombay" had higher claims on Jamsetjee than the enchanting Khandalla as regards a Dharamsala. To an English Reader, who is unacquainted with Indian life, it will appear strange why the seat of Government, the emporium of commerce, where all who are willing to work can get a fair day's wages, and where there are so many rich and benevolent men, should have a place especially set apart for the Labitation of the poor. But England is not Bombay. It has no parishes where pious clergymen, generous ladies, and benevolent laymen look after the welfare of the poor, frequent their houses, play with their children, and assist them in person at the time of calamity. Here the rich are perfectly indifferent to the happiness of the poor; they merely pay them for their work, and think no more about them. They think it perfectly below their dignity to allow a servant to approach their person, and instead of pitying their condition, they regard them with dislike. But if we ponder well on the subject we shall come to the conclusion that in this they are but little to blame. The constitution of society here is so heterogeneous, that we cannot expect the slightest sympathy for the poor in the hearts of the rich. Difference in race, caste and religion is its sole cause. An European spurns from his sight a slovenly and miserable-looking Native, and never has the remotest idea of bettering his condition. Hence a Dharamsala was the greatest desideratum in Bombay. Nor were its claims left unsatisfied. Seeing the working of the District Benevolent Society inadequate for want of funds, Jamsetjee undertook to build a large house near Byculla, sufficient to afford a commodious habitation to three hundred persons, the poor of every caste and creed. The building was completed at an expense of eighty-five thousand Rupees, and opened to the public with great splendour on the 5th May, 1847. To provide for the maintenance of the poor who might take shelter there, Jamsetjee set apart a sum of seventy-thousand Rupees, and entrusted them to Government. This work is a remarkable proof of the interest that Jamsetjee took in the welfare of a class, which has no mouth-piece in India to claim its rights and privileges.

Like a current that gently glides in the beginning, but as it approaches the ocean expands in size, even so the stream of Jamsetjee's charity began to enlarge itself in its smooth course. The thirsty he had supplied with water; the religious he had supplied with fire-temples; the debtors he had supplied with money; and the poor he had supplied with food and clothing. Now remained two great works for him to perform:—a suitable building for the infirm and the sick, and one for the education of his countrymen. The former first engaged his attention. In 1834, a small hospital near the verge of the Esplanade was opened by contributions, and the well-known Dr. Mackey here gave his advice to the poor. Four years elapsed, and then the worthy Doctor called a meeting of the subscribers and the notabilities of the land, and there read a report of the proceedings of the Hospital. Amongst others, Jamsetjee was present at the meeting. He was intensely gratified with the report, and thought the institution worthy of support. But seeing that the poor had no accommodation while sick for remaining in the Hospital itself, he proposed and asked the Chairman of the meeting, Sir Herbert Compton, to correspond in his name with Government, and convey to them his wishes of building an extensive Hospital in Bombay where three hundred persons might with comfort be accommodated. He promised to give a lac of Rupees for this purpose, on condition that Government would contribute an equal amount, as well as appropriate to the expenses of the new Hospital, the sum of three hundred Rupees they were contributing every month to the old one. This idea was a noble one, and a Committee was at once formed, headed by Mr. J. H. Crawford, the sincere friend of Jamsetjee, to correspond with Government on the subject. In a letter dated the 3rd. of April, 1838, the Committee conveyed to Government the wishes of Jamsetjee. The proposal was sent through Bengal to the Home Government, with strong recommendations from them. It was accepted by the Court of Directors with hearty good will, and their thanks were communicated to Jamsetjee by Mr. Morris the Secretary, in a letter dated the 11th. of November, 1840, and enclosed therein was a copy of a Resolution of Government, to the effect that the building be called the "Sir Jamsetjee Jeejeebhoy's Hospital," and that a part of it be set apart for those who bring a recommendation from Jamsetjee or his heirs. The management was also left in the hands of Jamsetjee and his heirs, who were to be assisted by two gentlemen appointed by Government. Jamsetjee was greatly pleased with this; he returned his thanks to Government, at the same time intimating that he had purchased a site for the Hospital for a sum of twenty four thousand one hundred and twenty five Rupees. He also promised to increase his original donation of ten thousand Rupees for the building of the Hospital to fifty thousand Rupees. Government were agreeably surprised at this fresh instance of his munificence, and lost no time in conveying to him their appreciation of his generous nature.

And now the auspicious day for laying the foundation stone of the Hospital was appointed. It was the 3rd. of January, 1843. The sun is now approaching the horizon, the hourhand points to four, and the rattling of horses and carriages begins. The Garrison Band now enlivens the scene and with its mellifluous tone enchants the solitary Mazagon. Now comes the Governor with Jamsetjee and staff; then follows the gallant MacMohun in his warlike costumes and after him tread with gravity and state the pious band of Freemasons* in the following order:—
Two Tylers with drawn Swords.
Brethren not attached to the Lodges, two and two.
The Lodge "Perseverance" of Bombay, two and two.
Asst. Wardens, Brs. A. LARKWORTHY and H. GREED.
V. W. Br. H. J. BARR, Master.
The Provincial Grand Steward's Lodge, two and two.
Wardens, Brs. W. K. FOGERTY and J. M'CLEOD.

---

* This was the first occasion of a masonic display in Bombay.

V. W. Br. J. HARRISON.

The Architect of the Building,
Br. W. GOODFELLOW with the Plan.

Provincial Grand Guard,
W. Br. T. GARDINER with Wand.

Provincial Grand Marshalls,
V.W. Brs: J.S. UNWIN & A. WILSON, bearing Batons.

Provincial Grand Director of Ceremonies,
V. W. Br. J. S. LAWLESS with Cornucopia.

P. G. Superintendent of Works,
V. W. Br. R. FRITH with Mallet.

Past Provincial Grand Junior Deacon,
V. W. Br. C. A. WEST with Cup of Oil.

Past Provincial Grand Senior Deacon,
V. W. Br. W. PURNELL with Cup of Wine.

Provincial Grand Treasurer,
V. W. Br. W. W. CARGILL with Bottle of Coins.

Present & Past Provincial Grand Registrars,
V. W. Brs. R. M. KIM & W. HOWARD, with the Inscribed Plate.

Present & Past Provincial Grand Secretaries,
V. W. Brs. W. BLOWERS & SPENCER COMPTON, with the books of constitutions.

Past Provincial Grand Officers,
V. W. Brs. J. GLEN, C. B. SKINNER, T. VALIANT, K. H. J. SKINNER and J. GRIFFITH.

Past Grand Wardens,
R. W. Brs. J. P. WILLOUGHBY and W. CRAWFORD.

Junior Provincial Grand Warden,
R. W. Br. NEIL CAMPBELL, with the Plumb.

Senior Provincial Grand Warden,
R. W. Br. L. R. REID, with the Level.

V. W. Br. M. WILLOUGHBY with the Vol. of the Sacred Law.

Provincial Grand Chaplain,
V. W. Br. Geo. BUIST. LL. D.

Deputy Provincial Grand Master,
R. W. Br. P. W. LeGEYT, with the Square.

Provincial Grand Standard Bearers,
V. W. Brs. G. ROWLEY and E. DANVERS, with the banner of the P. G. M.

Offg. Provincial Grand Master,
R. W. Br. The Hon'ble G. W. ANDERSON, with the Silver Trowel.

Provincial Grand Sword Bearers,
V. W. Brs. J. BOYD and E. L. ARTHUR.

The Provincial Grand Master,
R. W. Br. J. BURNES K. H.

The P. G. Deacons in a line seven feet apart,
V. W. Brs. J. CHALMERS and H. B. HERRICK.

Provincial Grand Pursuivant,
V. W. Br. A. W. ELLIOT, with Wand.

P. Master of the Provincial Grand Stewards,
V. W. Br. E. A. FARQUHARSON.

Two P. G. Stewards, with Wands,
Brs: ECKFORD and J. W. RENNY.

Provincial Grand Guard,
W. Br. G. S. COLLETT, with Sword.

"On the Procession reaching the Ground, it halted, and faced inwards forming a broad line through which the Provincial Grand Master, and the Provincial and Deputy Provincial Grand Masters passed to the East of the Foundation-stone; Brothers L. Reid & J. Willoughby, taking their position on the West, and Brothers N. Campbell and W. Crawford on the South, and Sir Jamsetjee Jeejeebhoy, and his son, Cursetjee Jamsetjee Esquire, on the North of the stone. Music was then played, and the architect of the building presented the Plan to the Provincial Grand Master. The Registrar and Treasurer also presented the Inscribed Plate and the coins.

"The Plate, Plan and coins were then submitted to the Hon'ble the Governor, and Sir Jamsetjee Jeejeebhoy; and the Provincial Grand Master having expressed his gratification at His Excellency's presence, the Inscription on the Plate was read aloud by the Deputy Provincial Grand Master:—

In the Reign of
Her Most Gracious Majesty
VICTORIA;
And under the Government of
EDWARD, LORD ELLENBOROUGH
Governor General of India:
GEORGE MARQUIS of TWEEDLE K. T.
Being Governor of Madras:
and
The Hon'ble Sir GEORGE ARTHUR BART. K. C. H.
Governor of Bombay:
The Foundation stone of
The Jamsetjee Jeejeebhoy Hospital
was laid with Masonic Honours
in the presence of
SIR JAMSETJEE JEEJEEBHOY,
the Founder,
and of
His EXCELLENCY the GOVERNOR
by
JAMES BURNES, K. H.
Provincial Grand Master of Western India:
assisted by
The Hon'ble GEO. W. ANDERSON Pro. P. P. G. M.
P. W. LEGEYT Esquire D. P. G. M.
LESTOCK. R. REID Esq. P. G. S. W.
Lieut. Colonel, NEIL CAMPBELL. P. G. J. W.
Captain W. GOODFELLOW, the Architect
and a numerous convocation of the Craft,
On Tuesday, the third day of January,
In the year of the Christian Era, 1843,
and of Masonry, 5843

THE INSCRIPTION.

THIS EDIFICE

Was erected as a Testimonial of devoted loyalty to
the young Queen of the British Isles,
And of unmingled respect for the just and paternal
British Government in India ;
Also in affectionate and patriotic solicitude for the welfare
of the poor classes of all races among his countrymen.
The British subjects of Bombay;

by

SIR JAMSETJEE JEJEEBHOY, KNIGHT,
The first native of India honoured with British knighthood,
Who thus hopes to perform a pleasing duty
towards his Country, his Government, and his People;
And in solemn remembrance of blessings bestowed,
To present this,
his offering of Religious Gratitude, to
ALMIGHTY GOD,
The Father in Heaven
of the Christian, the Hindoo, the Mohammedan, & the Parsee.
With humble earnest prayer
for His continued care and blessing
upon his Children, his Family, his Tribe, and his Country.

"The Provincial Grand Master, the Provincial and Deputy Provincial Grand Masters, and the Grand Wardens, then descended into the trench, and the stone having been raised by the united aid of the Brethren, the Deputy Provincial Grand master deposited the coins and the Inscribed Plate in their respective places, and spread the cement with a trowel. After which the stone was lowered into its destined bed, conducted by the Deputy Provincial Grand master, and the Architect—Solemn music playing.

"The Provincial Grand master then addressed the Provincial Grand Officers—" Right Worshipful brethren, we shall now apply the various implements of our royal craft borne by you to this stone, that it may be laid in its bed according to the rules of Architecture, and in conformity with our ancient rite and usages." R. W. Junior G. Warden— " What is the emblem of your office " ? to which the reply was—" The plumb, R. W. Sir, which I now present for your use." The Level and Square having in like manner been presented by R. W. Bis. Reid and LeGeyt, the stone was proved by these implements by the P. G. Master, who pronounced it to be " Well-Formed, True and Trusty." The mallet was then handed by Brother Goodfellow to the P. G. Master, who delivered it to the R. W. Br. Anderson, who struck the stone with it thrice, and the P.-G. Master having also struck the stone three times, repeated the prayer. " May the Great Architect of the Universe grant a blessing on this stone which we have now laid, and enable us by

His Providence to finish this, and any other virtuous undertaking. Amen, so mote it be." The Grand officers and brethren gave the usual response and masonic honours. The Provincial grand Master then delivered the implements to the Architect and addressed him as follows:—" Brother William Goodfellow, the skill and fidelity displayed by you at the commencement of this undertaking have secured the entire approbation of your brethren, and they sincerely pray that the Jamsetjee Jeejeebhoy Hospital may be a lasting monument of your wisdom and taste, and of the noble spirit and the splendid liberality of its' founder" The Cornucopia and Cups of Wine & Oil were then presented by the respective bearers through the P. G. Wardens, a D. P. G. Master, to the P. G. Master, who having poured them on the stone, said;—" May the All bounteous Author of nature bless the inhabitants of this place with all the necessaries, conveniences and comforts of life; assist in the erection & completion of this building, protect the workmen against every accident, and long preserve this structure from decay. Amen, so mote it be"—The brethren again gave the usual response and the masonic honours.

Dr Burnes then addressed Sir Jamsetjee in the following terms:—

"Sir Jamsetjee Jeejeebhoy,

"Many and memorable have been the occasions on which the deeds of charitable and philanthrophic men have been consecrated by the ancient rites and ceremonies of our masonic craft, but never have those ceremonies been employed to aid a purpose more congenial to the feelings of the upright mason or the true hearted lover of his species than the present. The splendid structure which you here propose to dedicate to the relief of your fellow-creatures as well as many other transcendant acts of benevolence that have characterized your career, are like our Masonic Institution itself, kindred and goodly fruits of the most generous emotion that can swell the bosom of man towards man; the desire to succour his brother in distress and to give free scope to that ever hallowed charity

"Which droppeth as the gentle rain from Heaven,
And blesseth Him that gives and Him that takes"

It is with a cordial sympathy, therefore, as well as with sincere pride and gratification that the masonic fraternity of Bombay have responded to your summons, and borne their emblems to this spot today. And when the record of these Proceedings shall be read within the Houses of our Order dispersed throughout the civilized world, our brethren also, of every tongue and nation will rejoice that we have been aiding you in this good work, and will participate with us in exultation, that by far the foremost man for deeds of true wisdom in this portion of the globe, has also, in giving effect to munificent designs of love and charity, been the first of his tribe and country to solicit the countenance of our brotherhood.

It has been usual to explain these ceremonies, and in this, the first instance of their being practised at Bombay, it is essential that I should at least guard against their being misinterpreted. There is one portion of them which will awaken a sympathy in the bosom of every reflecting individual, even of this vast assemblage, composed though it be of men of all varieties of sects, customs and habits of thought, since no condition of Society exists, in which at the season of doubt and anxiety, but specially at the commencement of a momentous undertaking, the plan of which he may conceive, but the execution of which depends on a far mightier than he—man will not feel his absolute dependence upon the Omnipotent Creator, and by a natural instinct turn to His throne for support. And the impulse which prompts this appeal acquires intensity when the frail and transitory being contemplates the erection of an enduring and stupendous structure which may rear its stately head for centuries after he is mouldering in the dust and hence, from the remotest ages, and in almost all countries, the foundation-stone of important edifices has been deposited with an impressive solemnity, indicative of the founder's humble trust and fervent prayer, that the great Architect of the Universe may prosper his work, and ever shower down his bounty and blessings upon it. As visible types of those blessings, it has also been usual in accordance with a practice which needs no elucidation amongst a people long accustomed to shadow forth solemn truths by symbols and allegory—to pour forth with the spirit of hope and thankfulness, the abundant fruits of the earth on the first corner-stone in the corn of nourishment, the wine of refreshment, and the oil of joy. Such, then, is the simple origin of one portion of these ceremonies, which so far will be recoginsed as analogous to those performed by one of our most distinguished Parsee families in laying the foundation keels of some of those superb vessels which of late years have brought Great Britain and India into closer and dearer connexion.

The other part of the ceremony, I have more difficulty in explaining, not that it is less clear to myself, but that there are certain land-marks which I must not transgress, and within the strict limits of which, explanation may be embarassing. But I do not despair to render it also intelligible, and your character and conduct, my worthy friend, afford me scope for doing so. You have seen me then, apply certain implements of operative architecture to this stone, in accordance with the ancient and immemorial usage of our Order at the foundation of all stately and superb edifices. But you are too enlightened a man to suppose that the essence of Free Masonry lies in a mere formality like this, or that those about me and myself have linked ourselves together in an indissoluble tie, only to practise ceremonial or display. No! as the corn, the wine and the oil were symbols of God's bounty and providence, calling forth reverence and gratitude to the Creator, so also, even the Stone and implements are emblems conveying to the enlightened Mason, pure and precious precepts of his duty to his neighbour. They are, in truth, tokens of a great and practical system of universal good will and benevolence, which, establishing moral worth as the standard, welcomes to its bosom the good of every colour, clime or creed that acknowledges God, which binds you, whose name and deeds fill men's mouths, as those of the "benevolent Parsee of Bombay," and *longo intervallo,* myself, the child of Northern Europe, and all who are willing to work with us to "mitigate the sum of human woe," into one vast chain of fraternity and love; which enforces the most devout reverence to the Supreme Architect, and the strictest conscientious duty to our earthly rulers, but at the same time peremptorily excludes all discussions on points of faith, state politics, or other questions likely to excite the angry passions of Man against Man; and which in short is founded on the glorious principle that

"God hath made mankind one mighty brotherhood
Himself the Master, and the world their Lodge."

Many of those eminent individuals whose names are dearest to India, have been professors or promoters of this vast system. In the Right Worshipful Brother by my side* you will recognise one from whom even you have obtained encouragement, and who has with zeal and fervency devoted his gifts as a man, and his power as a Governor to the

---
* The Hon'ble Mr. G. W. Anderson.

dissemination of charity and enlightenment amongst your countrymen. The late Marquis of Hastings, certainly inferior to none of the illustrious men that Europe has lent to Asia was a stately pillar of our craft; and there is a valued and elevated brother present, who could testify how deeply its principles influenced the conduct of that distinguished soldier and statesman. The present ruler of India shewed his respect for it, by demanding, so late as 1836, that a legislative enactment should be so expressed as not reflect upon its members. We have lately seen the Government of a sister Presidency transferred from one noble brother to another, and if we cannot include amongst us, the distinguished officer who presides at Bombay, we have the satisfaction of seeing his son amongst our office bearers.

Through the mercy of Providence from the earliest period, the system I have described has been in operation, assuaging the horrors of strife and encouraging the spread of civilization, and while your remote forefathers were bowing with adoration to the glorious Orb of day, the visible source of light, heat and productiveness, our, ancient brethren, if they were, not identical with them, were also by the symbols of the Sun, the Moon and the

Starry Firmament, inculcating the mighty truth of God's power, omnipresence and divinity, and of man's responsibility, hope and final destiny, thereby evincing their sympathy and connection with those

> " Who morn and eve
> Hail their Creator's dwelling place
> Among the lights of Heaven."

I have said that your life and character afford scope for illustrating our system, and I now turn to my masonic brethren and present you to them as a brother who has practically attained the summit of the masonic structure, which is *Charity*. Never forgetting that you commenced and must end upon the *level*, following the *Plumb-line* of rectitude, acting on the *square* with your fellow-men, circumscribing your own wants within *compass*, but extending your benevolence to a *circle* which, if it depended upon you would evidently embrace all mankind; we need not wonder that you have attained the highest elevation of moral worth : that the love of your family, the respect of your fellow-citizens, the applause of men and rewards from your Sovereign, have flowed in upon you; and that, above all, you enjoy the serenity of mind arising from the inexpressible delight of having succoured the distressed,

" Which nothing earthly gives, or can destroy."

And although my friend, it has not fallen to us, who are, after all, but " nature's journeymen," to initiate you into our mysteries, we cannot doubt, after the splendid deeds of love wich you have achieved, that you are a wise Master Builder;—a living stone, squared, polished, fashioned, and proved by the hand of the Great Master himself— that your patent is from the Grand Chancery above, and that you need neither sign nor token, warrant nor diploma, pass-word nor grip, to ensure you a welcome to the heart of every honest mason.

May you, Sir Jamsetjee, like the foundation we have laid, long be stable and secure—may you, for years, be spared as the corner-stone of Charity, the prop and support of the widow and the fatherless;—may your good deeds form a constant source of enjoyment to yourself while you remain amongst men, and when the time does come that overtakes us all, and the solemn Tyler, Death, must raise the curtain of a new existence—may it be to usher you in, as an accepted and exalted companion, to the Supreme Chapter on high, there to take your place under the all-seeing eye of Him who seeth not as man seeth, but who will undoubtedly pay the workman his wages' according to his work." (Cheers)

Sir Jamsetjee replied as follows;—" Right Worshipful Sir, I feel beyond measure gratified that you and your masonic brethren have attended on this occasion to do so much honour to the foundation of the Hospital, which it is here proposed to erect. I was most desirous to obtain the countenance of your fraternity, because to say nothing of the regard and esteem I entertain for yourself and many of my valued friends whom I see supporting you, I have heard of its great antiquity, its universal benevolence, its toleration; and I know also that its objects are those of pure charity to all mankind. I have no language to express myself in return for the observations you have made of myself, but I trust I shall ever retain the good will and favorable opinion of my friends. I have also cordially to thank Sir George Arthur, Sir Thomas Mc Mohun and the many ladies and gentlemen whom I see here, for their attendance, which I cannot but feel, evinces on their part a deep interest in this new institution, which is most gratifying to me."

Amidst cheers Sir Jamsetjee ended; and the company then separated. The Hospital has cost him in all a sum of two lacs of Rupees. Its annual expenses amount to nearly thirty three thousand Rupees. A splendid clock is placed in one of its steeples, which at every hour reminds the neighbourhood of the charities of the venerable Sir Jamsetjee.

Now,

> The seeds of Knowledge he did sow,
> He bade grim Darkness then to go;
> Grim Darkness went and Knowledge came,
> And blotted out his India's shame.

The Education of the children of his castefellows drew Jamsetjee's attention next. The necessaries of man in his primæval state he had supplied them with, but real happiness ends not with the comforts of the body, but soars higher, and makes its abode principally in the regions of the intellect. Jamsetjee's sole aim and wish was to contribute as much as possible to their felicity—felicity of mind and felicity of body—and mould them not only into happy beings but clever citizens. Education, he thought, would awake them to a sense of their duties towards God and Man, spur them on to action, and teach them Love, Hope, and Patience.

> " O'er wayward childhood wouldst thou hold firm rule,
> And sun thee in the light of happy faces ;
> *Love, Hope,* and *Patience,* these must be thy graces,
> And in thine own heart let them first keep school.
> For as old Atlas on his broad neck places
> Heaven's starry globe, and there sustains it, so

> Do these upbear the little world below
> Of *Education—Patience, Love*, and *Hope*.
> Methinks I see them grouped in seemly show,
> The straitened arms upraised, the palms aslope,
> And robes that touching as adown they flow,
> Distinctly blend, like snow embossed in snow.
> O part them never ! If *Hope* prostrate lie
>   *Love* too will sink and die.
> But *Love* is subtle and doth proof derive
> From her own life that *Hope* is yet alive;
> And bending o'er, with soul transfusing eyes,
> And the soft murmurs of the mother-dove,
> Woos back the fleeting spirit, and half supplies;
> Thus *Love* repays to *Hope* what *Hope* first gave to *Love*.
> Yet haply there will come a weary day,
>   When overtasked at length
> But *Love* and *Hope* beneath the load give way.
> Then with a statue's smile, a statue's strength,
> Stands the mute sister, *Patience*, nothing loath,
> And both supporting, does the work of both."

But apart from its moral advantages, Education raises man from the mire of Ignorance in which he is stuck, and wiping off the dirt of Boorishness, makes him tread the decent road of Knowledge whose terminus is Happiness. Approaching which,

> " With sense to feel, with memory to retain,
> They follow pleasure, and they fly from pain ;
> Their judgment mends the plan their fancy draws,
> The event presages, and explores the cause;
> The soft returns of gratitude they know ;
> By fraud elude, by force repel the foe;
> While mutual wishes mutual woes endear,
> The social smile and sympathetic tear."

Keenly alive to these beneficial results, made more patent by the example of the dominant race, Jamsetjee thought of opening schools in all parts of

Bombay and Gujrat. With this view, he in 1843, * set apart a fund of four lacs and forty thousand Rupees to establish Schools in Bombay, Surat, Odepore, Nowsari, Broach and their adjacent provinces for both boys and girls. The schools are all in a very healthy state, particularly the Central School in Bombay, which through the industry and zeal of such able men as the late lamented Professsor Green, and our learned Dr. Fraser and the present Principal Mr. Burgess has gained a good name. It is now one of the feeders of our young University, and we are glad to say that five of its students have passed in the last Matriculation Examination. The Government Educational Inspector annually examines it, and the last report is very satisfactory. About 1800 boys and 1200 girls take advantage of these schools. We hope, however, that its supervisors will soon see that an efficient staff of assistant masters is appointed, as the present one is miserably inadequate. To " teach the young idea how to shoot " is the task of a clever man, and not of an half-educated youth.

Besides these princely charities which are patent to all, there are others no less conspicuous. Jam-

---

* For a full account of the circumstances attending the origin of this donation see Chapter IX.

setjee gave a lac and twentyfive thousand Rupees towards a Fund which was raised to relieve the miseries of the poor in Surat. For a similar purpose in Nowsari, he contributed the large sum of sixty thousand, five hundred Rupees. At an expense of twenty thousand Rupees he built a Dharamsala and a public garden in Nowsari. He also paid to the Guicwar the handsome sum of (17000) seventeen thousand Rupees, to redeem the poor Parsis of Nowsari from the body tax. To the fund raised to support the poor Parsis of Bombay, he gave a sum of (15000) fifteen thousand Rupees. In the erection of towers of silence and firetemples (others than those before mentioned) he spent a sum of (47,000) forty-seven thousand Rupees. To keep alive the memory of his junior partner and friend, Motichund Amichund, he instituted a fund in his name by a contribution of thirty thousand Rupees, which were to be used for the relief of poor Banians in Gujrat. Towards the Institution established by the "mild Hindoos" of Bombay and Patan, he gave the handsome sum of 74,600 Rupees. In giving support to poor but formerly respectable families, he disburdened himself of forty-four thousand Rupees. At an expense of (33,000) thirty-three thousand Rupees he built tanks at Bandora and Byculla. He also founded at an expense of the munificent sum of one lac of Rupees, a school of arts and science, which is now known as the Sir Jamsetjee Jeejeebhoy's School of Arts and Science. This is an invaluable institution in Bombay, and under the able guidance of Mr. Terry it has distinguished itself. Some of its scholars are now excellent painters and designers. He also established a dispensary at Nowsari for a sum of seventy-five thousand Rupees. To the Professorships' fund of the Elphinstone College, he contributed a sum of (11500) eleven thousand five hundred Rupees. To the prize fund of the Grant Medical College he subscribed fifteen thousand Rupees. In building other wells, causeways, a * firetemple in Bombay, and roads leading to the Towers of Silence in Bombay and Nowsari he spent in all a sum of one lac and twenty two thousand Rupees. To support the poor carpenters of the Dockyard, and in subscriptions to the Byculla Schools, Sailor's Home, Shivry School of Industry, Calcutta Free School, the naval school at Davenport, Wellington Testimonial, Patriotic Fund, Relief Fund, Havelock Testimonial, and in sundry other contributions he spent about a lac and fifty thousand Rupees.

---

* Built after his death.

These handsome benefactions amount to an aggregate sum of about twenty-three lacs and eighty-six thousand Rupees,—benefactions which have been surpassed by none of all climes and ages. Millionaires there have been many in all countries, who in point of wealth have surpassed Jamsetjee, in honesty and integrity equalled him, but none has up to this time dared to approach him in the magnanimity that dictated these munificent donations. And the sum total mentioned above refers only to his public acts of charity, so when we take into consideration the

"Deeds

"Above heroic, though in secret done,"
his private gifts, we cannot but wonder at the noble nature of the heart whence this stream of benevolence took its rise. And as deeds of charity were in his time but "few and far between" in India, their fame spread throughout the land and reached the ears of our monarch. Herself being a votary to the goddess of charity, she fully appreciated the catholic and philanthropic nature of his acts of benevolence, and bestowed on him titles which reflect undiminishing lustre both on the fair giver and the modest taker, and of which we reserve an account for the next chapter.

CHAPTER VIII.

And now devolves upon us the most pleasing task of all. Charities like those we have enumerated must command the admiration of mankind, and cannot fail to rouse a spirit of gratitude and esteem in the breasts of all who observe and profit by them. And thanks to the Almighty, men like these were not wanting in the world at the time. Sir James Carnac, who was for a long time Governor of Bombay, and who was ever a careful observer of the good deeds of Jamsetjee, on his return to England through illness in 1841, represented to the Court of Directors, and through them to our gracious Sovereign, the benefactions of the benevolent Parsee. He drew a touching picture of the good old man, who passing through so many and so great trials, as would have cowed a less indomitable spirit, had emerged from them with a heart tutored to feel for another's woes, distributing his bounty freely to men of every caste and creed, and like a true philanthropist relieving their wants and alleviating their miseries. He conveyed to them an idea of his magnificent works completed and under construction, and exhorted them to bestow on him some substantial proof of their appreciation of his worth.

Our then young Queen was much pleased with the news of the benefactions and high moral worth of one of Her Indian subjects, and as her first mark of favour she made him a Knight of the United Kingdom of Great Britain and Ireland. The welcome news was immediately conveyed to Jamsetjee on the 10th March, 1842. Oh the blessed 10th! What, Jamsetjee made a Knight? An Indian, a descendant of the race that was driven out by the bloody Mahomedans from Persia, who sought refuge in the cities of the "mild Hindoo," and eventually took shelter under the British Power, made a Knight? Yes!

> The first and only Indian Knight,
> By grace of England's virtuous Queen;
> She treated him with honour bright,
> Brightest of all his heart was seen.

Ay! his heart was the brightest, his soul the noblest, and his reward the meetest:—the reward which bravery, statesmanship, education, and lastly philanthropy obtain. And the auspicious day on which the news disclosed itself to him was a day celebrated in gaiety and mirth by his family and friends. Nor was the happiness theirs only, for all India now raised its head on high, and the Indian Elephant began to walk as it were with reassuring confidence that India's well-being is cared for by the Home authorities, and that the good of all caste gain an equal share of praise at the hands of the Queen.

And now an official despatch came from the Court of Directors to Sir George Anderson, bidding him communicate to Jamsetjee the title he had obtained and to publicly bear testimony to his worth. The glorious 25th of May, the birthday of our most gracious Sovereign, was selected by Sir George for this grand ceremony. The Government House, at Parell was gaily adorned for the occasion with festoons and evergreens.

"Sir Jamsetjee, arrived at half past ten o'clock, when he was conducted from the entrance Hall to the reception room, attended by Henry Lacon Anderson, Esquire, the private Secretary, on one hand, and Major Willoughby, the military Secretary on the other, preceded by a large body of *chopdars* and state peons. On arriving at the top of the Grand Room, he was met by the Hon'ble the Governor, who was supported by His Excellency the Commander-in-chief, and the heads of Departments. The patent of Knighthood lay on a damask cushion in front of the Governor, who after heartily and most cordially greeting Sir Jamsetjee, proceeded to address him in the following terms:—

" Sir Jamsetjee Jeejeebhoy—Her most Gracious

Majesty the Queen having been graciously pleased to confer upon you the dignity of Knight of the United Kingdom, the Patent has been transmitted to me to present to you, and both Lord Fitzgerald, the President of the Board of Control—and the Hon'ble the Court of Directors in transmitting this instrument to me for this purpose have expressed their high gratification at your having received this distinguished honour.

The dignity of Knighthood has ever amongst the natives of Europe been considered as most honorable. To attain this distinction has continually been the ambition of the highest minds and noblest spirits, either by deeds of the most daring valour, or by the exercise of the most eminent talent.

You, by your deeds for the good of mankind, by your acts of Princely munificence to alleviate the pains of suffering humanity, have attained this honour and have become enrolled amongst the illustrious of the land.

This honour of which you may be so justly proud, cannot fail at the same time of being highly satisfactory to your fellow countrymen, who in this distinguished mark of Her Majesty's gracious favour to you, must see how equal is the consideration Her Majesty extends to all classes of Her subjects, and that where deeds worthy of honour are done, upon all will honour be conferred, how different soever the race, or distant the country of Her Realm.

To me who have so long known you, and have so long and fully appreciated your truly estimable character, it is most pleasing that it should have fallen to my hands to present you with this Patent of Knighthood. I present it—congratulating you most sincerely upon the distinction and honour which your worth has achieved."

At the conclusion of the address, the Band struck up the National Anthem, and Sir Jamsetjee replied as follows:—

" Sir,

I am unable to express my feelings on receiving so gratifying a proof of Her most gracious Majesty's favour as being raised to the high distinction of the Knighthood of the United Kingdom:—an honour most unlooked for, yet doubly acceptable from the gracious manner in which it has been announced and conferred upon me. I cannot, Sir, nor will I attempt to look back upon the causes which have drawn on me Her Majesty's approbation and its consequent honours, but I can honestly declare I looked not for such rewards, but felt satisfied in being able, out of the abundance which a gracious Providence had bestowed upon me, to spare something towards mitigating the sufferings of my less fortunate fellow-creatures; still I feel a high, I hope a justifiable, pride in the distinction of being enrolled in the Knighthood of England marked as that order has ever been by the brightest traits of loyalty and honour. But these honours are gratifying to me not only in a personal view as being the first native of India on whom they have been conferred, but as they bear also upon my own people and my fellow countrymen in general, as a pledge that we are not uncared for, but that on the throne of England our loyalty and devotion are appreciated. This conviction must lead to good, for it cannot fail to act as a spur to future exertions that we know, distant as we are, we are not hidden from the ever watchful and maternal eye of our beloved Sovereign.

But I feel I should be wanting in gratitude were I not to tender my warmest acknowledgments to the Hon'ble the Court of Directors, the Rulers of this mighty Empire, for the kind and cordial interest they have taken on my behalf and for their recommendation to Her Majesty's Ministers, to which I am mainly indebted for the notice of our most gracious Sovereign—the source of all honour. And together with my acknowledgments I would assure that Hon'ble Board that their native subjects fully appreciate the anxious endeavours they have made to ameliorate their condition, and lead them, step by step, to the full enjoyments of the blessings of the British constitution and the honours of their English brethren.

' If there is anything which could enhance the value of Her most gracious Majesty's approbation I feel it to be, Sir, that the honours my Sovereign has been pleased to bestow upon me, have been presented through one I have so long known, esteemed and honoured as yourself; and I must beg of you, Sir, to accept my' most hearty acknowledgments and thanks for the marked and distinguished manner in which you have been pleased to express your sentiments and congratulations in conferring those honours upon me."

The most hearty plaudits followed Sir Jamsetjee's address and his numerous friends present pressed forward to congratulate the new-made Knight, who received the courtesies offered him in his usual kindly and hearty manner, and but one feeling appeared to prevail in the whole assembly, that of hearty goodwill to the man who stood before them, the honoured of his Sovereign. At supper, the Hon'ble the Governor proposed the health of the first knight of India—Sir Jamsetjee Jeejeebhoy—with three times three cheers, which was drank with the greatest enthusiasm. The party did not separate till a late hour of the evening, or rather early next morning."—

CHAPTER IX.

But the demonstrations of joy did not end here. Not to be behindhand in honouring the man who was honoured by his sovereign, the native friends of Sir Jamsetjee proposed to present him with an address, and with this view they appointed the 15th June as the auspicious day—On that day, they, in company with the European friends of Sir Jamsetjee repaired to his mansion in the Fort. A detailed account of the occasion we quote from the "Bombay Times" of that period.

Princely munificence of Sir Jamsetjee Jeejeebhoy.—

On the forenoon of Wednesday last, a very numerous party of European and Parsee gentlemen assembled at the mansion of Sir Jamsetjee Jeejeebhoy, to witness the presentation of an address to him by his kinsmen and friends, accompanied by a testimonial, value Rs 15,000 (i.e. £ 1,500). Nearly all the distinguished members of the Parsee community were present; and amongst the Europeans we observed the Hon'ble Mr. Anderson, Major General D. Barr; Major General T. Valiant; A. Bell, G. Gilberne and B. Hutt Esquires, Judges of the Sudder Adawlut; W. R. Morris, Esq., Secretary to Government; Colonel J. H Dunsterville; Colonel S. Hughes, C. B; W. C. Bruce Esquire, Accountant General; A. Spens Esq, C. S; Colonel Dickinson; Captain Oliver, R. N; Captain Ross, I. N; E. E. Elliot Esq, C. S: the Hon'ble Captain West, A. D. C. to the Governor; Captain Arthur; H. L. Anderson Esquire, C. S; Captain M. Willoughby; Dr. J. Burnes, K. H. Secretary Medical Board; P. W. LeGeyt, C. S; James Matheson; H. Fawcett, R. Crawford, John Bowman, C. B. Skinner, G. Buist and J. G. Malcomson, Esquires; Dr. W. Mackie; Sir Roger de Faria, &c,&c.

The shape in which the testimonial was given might well put to shame the gifts of pictures, statues, and silver plate which too often constitute similar memorials in Europe: the sum already named (£ 1, 500) constitute a fund for the purpose of procuring translations into Goozeratee (the language of the Parsees) of the best European or Asiatic Works, ancient and modern; and generally for the institution of schools and promotion of knowledge; and

F

the relief of the sick and indigent natives. This was
so far excellent: but when Sir Jamsetjee thanked
his friends for their kindness, as well as for the
manner in which it was exhibited, he stated that
he would add three lacks of Rupees (£ 30,000
Sterling!!) to the sum subscribed, the whole to be
devoted under the designation of "The Jamsetjee
Jeejeebhoy Fund" to the purposes notified in the address to him:—this we will venture to say is, under the
circumstances, an instance of princely munificence
nearly unparalleled. Sir Jamsetjee Jeejeebhoy was
a private native merchant still in the full spring
tide of prosperous business; the founder of his
own fortunes, who never held place of profit
under government; who moreover, so far from
being in the act of disposing of a fortune on the
brink of the grave without heirs or claimants was
in enjoyment of full vigour of body and mind in
a green old age, with a large and talented
family brought up in a manner befitting their
station, who all of them most heartily and cordially
concur in this alienation, for the public good, of a
part of that princely heritage which would otherwise
be their own, and of which there still seems residue
enough for the wishes of the most ambitious. . Sir
Jamsetjee had, within these three or four years bes-

towed on public charities altogether independently of private benefactions sums which conjointly amount to upwards of five lakhs of Rupees or nearly £ 50,000 Sterling !!

The party already noticed having been assembled, Framjee Cowasjee Esq. spoke as follows:—

Sir Jamsetjee Jeejeebhoy.—We are assembled to present you an address of congratulation on the occasion of your having been selected by our revered Sovereign for the high and distinguished honour of Knighthood. Your merits are so well known, and your eminent virtues so well understood, that it is needless for me to say one word on the subject. In consideration of the presence of our European friends, I have to request that you will permit the address to be read in English by our friend Bomonjee Hormusjee, Esquire.

This request having been acceded to, the following address was read by that gentleman.

To Sir Jamsetjee Jeejeebhoy, Knight,

Sir,

We the undersigned Parsee and Hindoo inhabitants of Bombay, would not be doing justice to our feelings, or those of the community to which we belong, were we on an occasion like the present, to withhold the expression of our deep sense of the gracious condescension and benevolent regard evinced by Her Majesty the Queen towards Her most faithful subjects in the country by conferring on a Native of India the rank, dignity, and privileges of a Knight of the British Realm or were we to omit offering to you our sincere congratulations on your receiving so honorable a token of Her Majesty's approbation, of your wellknown public spirit and generous application of the means placed by Providence at your disposal to works of public utility, and objects connected with the comfort, welfare and happiness of Her Majesty's subjects in this Presidency.

Though you are the first Native on whom such a high honour has been conferred and though the first instance of the acts and conduct of a Native of British India attracting the favorable notice of our Sovereign it is impossible not to concur in the justice of the sentiment which has already so generally manifested itself that Her Majesty's present act will strengthen and confirm the feelings of loyal attachment towards her person and Government of Her Native subjects throughout the length and breadth of this Her extensive Indian Empire: while a strong incentive will be created, which we are convinced will be generally felt to emulate those good deeds for which you have been so distinguished.

When we consider that but a few years ago when it was proposed to render Natives eligible to serve on the Grand Jury, and to hold commissions as Justices of the Peace, the measure was opposed at the India House by all the Directors except one, the late excellent Governor Sir James Carnac, our much esteemed and lamented friend Mr. John Forbes, and the present Chairman Mr. G. Lyall, and was at length carried only by the untiring and philanthropic exertion of the then President of the Board of Control, Lord Glenelg, aided by other distinguished friends of India, and contrast this with (what we understand to be) the fact that the proposal to confer on you the honour of Knighthood was unanimously supported by the Hon'ble Body, we cannot but rejoice at the change of feeling from that then evinced towards the Natives of this country. We hail it as the harbinger of a brighter day for India when Britain shall no longer view her dominions here as a means of aggrandizement for her own sons, but as a sacred trust, of which the paramount object is the welfare of the children of the soil and the improvement and elevation of their moral and social condition.

We shall not expatiate upon your princely donation of a Lac and fifty thousand Rupees towards the foundation of an Hospital for all classes of the community—your munificent offer to Government to contribute (50,000) fifty Thousand Rupees towards the construction of a causeway or Vellard at Mahim to connect Bombay and Salsette—the construction of a spacious building at Khandallah on the high road to the Deccan for the accommodation of travellers; nor upon the prompt and liberal relief which from your own purse and through your personal exertions, has been afforded to your fellow creatures in distress, especially on the two occasions in which the city of Surat was visited with extensive and calamitous fires; while in your private charities, your hand has ever been ready to alleviate the sufferings of the widow and the orphan, the unfortunate and the destitute: there are few public institutions at this Presidency which have not shared largely in your bounty. Neither is it necessary to dwell upon the benefit which the trade of this port has derived from the enterprise and magnitude of your commercial operations, nor to point out the great extent to which you have availed yourself of the means of doing good derived from your mercantile knowledge and experience, joined to a conciliatory disposition and the probity of your character, as well as from your position in the Native Community by arranging differences, and settling disputes, so as to save the parties from the evils of a tedious and expensive litigation. But we would allude to these circumstances merely to show the grounds of the high estimation in which you are universally held and of the feelings which have induced us to express our gratification at the distinction which has been conferred upon you:—a gratification which derives no small addition from the consideration of your being one of the principal members of our own Community.

To commemorate this auspicious event, we request your permission to apply a sum of money which we have subscribed towards forming a fund to be designated the "Sir Jamsetjee Jeejeebhoy's Translation Fund," to be vested in trustees for the purpose of being appropriated to defraying the expenses of translating into the Guzeratee language, such books from the European and Asiatic languages, whether ancient or modern, as may be approved of by the Committee, to be by them published and distributed gratis, or at a low price, among the Parsee Community in furtherance of the

Education of our people, of which you have ever been a warm friend and zealous patron."

After this, the following in the name of the native inhabitants of Poona and its vicinity, was read by Jeejeebhoy Dadabhoy, Esquire.

"Sir Jamsetjee Jeejeebhoy, Knight—It is with feelings of pleasure that I present to you six addresses from the Natives of Poona, Nugger, Sattara, Jalna, Ahmednugger and Hydrabad transmitted to me for the purpose of expressing to you the respect in which your talents and benevolence are held by them, and to congratulate you upon the high honour which Her most gracious Majesty the Queen of England has conferred upon you.

I should, Sir Jamsetjee, read the addresses, but as there are present several European gentlemen who know but little of the language in which they are written, were I to read then they would find it tedious. I am confident, Sir Jamsetjee, you will excuse my further complying with the request of these who have deputed me to present them to you than to express to you my sincere and heartfelt sympathy in the sentiments they contain."

The cheering with which these addresses were received by the party having subsided, Sir Jamsetjee spoke as follows :—

"My dear friends—I feel deeply gratified to you for the address which you have just presented to me: so distinguished a mark of the esteem of my fellow countrymen is an honour of which I and those who are most dear to me may justly be proud. To have been selected by my Sovereign as the Native through whom she was graciously pleased to extend the order of Knighthood to Her Indian subjects was, and ever must be a source of deep personal gratification to myself. But to receive the congratulations of my fellow countrymen in a manner at once so kind and flattering, to have this auspicious event commemorated by the creation of a charity to be connected with my name and in the objects of which I so cordially concur, is a source of inward pride and satisfaction, which rising higher than the gratification of mere worldly titles, will live with me to my dying day.

Your too kind and favorable mention of my acts of charity has much affected me. The only merit I have a right to claim for them is, that they proceeded from a pure and heartfelt desire, out of the abundance with which Providence has blessed me, to ameliorate the condition of my fellow creatures. With this, no unworthy motive was mixed; I sought neither public honours nor private applause; and conscious of a singleness of purpose, I have long since had my reward. When, therefore, Her Majesty's most gracious intentions were communicated to me, I felt deeply gratified that I had unconsciously been the means of exciting so signal a mark of the good feelings of England towards the people of India and it is in this light that I prefer to consider the distinguished honour Her Majesty has conferred upon me, and that also which I have received at your hands this day.

Nothing could please me more than the purposes to which you propose to devote the funds that have been subscribed. I shall ever wish my name to be connected with every endeavour to diffuse knowledge amongst our people; and the surest way to incite them to elevate and improve themselves, to fit them to appreciate the blessings of the Government under which they live, and to deserve those honours, which have now, for the first time, been extended to India, is to spread far and wide amongst them, gratuitously or in a cheap form, translations into our own language of the works of the most approved authors. Connected with this subject is a scheme that I have long contemplated, for relieving the distresses of the Parsee poor of Bombay, Surat and its neighbourhood. You know full well the state of misery in which many of our people are living, and the hopeless ignorance in which their children are permitted to grow up. My object is to create a fund, the interest of which shall be applied towards relieving the indigent of our people, and the education of their children, and I propose to invest the sum of 300,000 Rupees in the public securities, and to place it at the disposal of trustees, who with the interest, shall carry out the object I have mentioned, and this trust I hope you will take under your care.

And now, my dear friends, let me once again thank you for your kindness. There is nothing I value so highly as the good opinion of my countrymen; nor anything I more anxiously desire than their welfare and happiness.

Jeejeebhoy Dadabhoy, I must beg of you to convey to the Native inhabitants of Poona, Ahmednugger, Sattara, Jalna, Aurungabad and Hyderabad, my warmest and most grateful thanks for the great honour they have done me in the addresses which I receive from your friendly hands. Assure them of my warmest interest and of my anxious desire to co-operate with them in all that may tend to improve their condition and add to their happiness.

The favour they have done me is greatly enhanced by your being selected to present the addresses in which they convey by far too flattering an expression of their feelings towards me. By the blessing of God and the support of many warm friends I have received a distinguished mark of favour from the Sovereign of England, I of course feel flattered and proud of the distinction conferred upon me, but no merely personal feeling of gratification would have given me the delight I experience in the kindly feeling towards India and her children evinced in the late gracious act of our beloved Sovereign.

Pray do me the favor, Jeejeebhoy, to convey to one and all of those who have signed the addresses my best and most cordial good wishes for their health, their happiness and their prosperity."

Thunders of applause followed this speech, and all hearts were so enchanted with the calmness with which three lacs were given away, that they felt as it were in a dream and exclaimed, Bravo! Sir Knight!!

Besides these, many more addresses poured in from all parts of Guzerat, all of which were replied to by Sir Jamsetjee in his usual modest manner.

The following is a description of his Coat of Arms :—

"Sir Jamsetjee Jeejeebhoy's "coat of arms" consists of a handsome shield in the form of the shields used by the Knights of St. John at the defence of Malta, beautifully emblazoned by scrolls of gold. At the lower part of the shield is a landscape scene in India, intended to represent a part of the island of Bombay, with the islands of Salsette and Elephanta in the distance. The sun is seen rising from behind Salsette to denote Industry, and in diffusing its light and heat displaying Liberality. The upper part of the shield has a white ground to denote Integrity and Purity, on which are placed two bees representing Industry and Perseverance. The shield is surmounted by a crest consisting of a beautiful peacock, denoting Wealth, Grandeur and Magnificence; and in its mouth is placed an ear of paddy, denoting Beneficence. Below the shield is a white pennant folded, on which is inscribed the words "INDUSTRY and LIBERALITY" which is Sir Jamsetjee's motto."

CHAPTER X.

But formal addresses were quite inadequate to

the worth of Sir Jamsetjee and so the Bombayites thought of a more substantial monument of his glory and greatness. The tribute which points out to futurity the heroic and good deeds of warriors and philanthropists, which reminds us now of Malcolm and Forbes, Wellesley and Elphinstone, was now marked out for him. The friends of Sir Jamsetjee now desired to erect a statue to his memory, and place it side by side with the conquerors of India. With this view a meeting of the inhabitants, both Native and European, of Bombay was called in June 1856. The chair was occupied by the excellent Lord Elphinstone, our late lamented worthy Governor, and the Town Hall was crowded to overflowing. Many were the excellent speeches made on this occasion in praise of Sir Jamsetjee, of which we cannot but quote in their integrity the speeches of Lord Elphinstone and of our late Chief Secretary to Government, the Hon'ble H. L. Anderson. Lord Elphinstone said:—

"When I was asked to preside over this meeting, I felt no ordinary satisfaction in accepting the invitation. The occasion was unusual, I believe I may say, in India, unprecedented. Every one must approve of the object so far, that every one must wish to do honour to Sir Jamsetjee Jeejeebhoy. Those who take an interest in the improvement and progress of the Natives of this country must, I think, view our proceedings to-day with peculiar pleasure. It is a good sign when a Community comes forward of its own accord to do homage to real worth; in honouring Sir Jamsetjee Jeejeebhoy, the Community honours itself. The mere fact of this meeting renders it superfluous that I should expatiate upon Sir Jamsetjee Jeejeebhoy's claims to our respect and love. But I would point out that these do not rest solely upon the vast sums which he has contributed to objects of public charity and convenience. The extent indeed, of those contributions is almost incredible; to enumerate the various benefits which he has conferred not only upon this town, but upon the Presidency at large, would be to trespass unduly upon your time. I may, however, be permitted to observe that his public benefactions alone amount to a quarter of a million sterling—or exactly the sum which it will take to construct the great works which will supply this island with water. In what age, and in what country, can we find another example of such princely munificence? Three of the largest cities in Great Britain, Glasgow, Liverpool and Manchester whose united population, however is not double that of Bombay,—have lately incurred, or are at this moment incurring an expense of upwards of two millions sterling upon waterworks. I will suppose that the united wealth of these three cities exceeds that of Bombay in the proportion that the cost of their water works bears to ours. I must admit that this is no criterion at all, and that it is very probable that I have much underrated their superiority of wealth—but which of these cities I ask, can boast of a citizen who has devoted 250,000 £s. to purposes of public charity and benevolence?

"But I have just said it is not the amount only of Sir Jamsetjee Jeejeebhoy's charities that commands my admiration. True liberality is shown in the manner of distribution no less than in the amount. I will not go back to the dark ages and cite the times when Christian monasteries and Buddhist Wickaras were endowed by men, who sought to gain the favour of Heaven by renouncing their possessions and performing what they considered an act of charity, and which was certainly one of abnegation. I may, however, refer to those who founded our great collegiate institutions, and to the monarch who built the Hotel des Invalides at Paris, and Greenwich and Chelsea Hospitals near London. The former afforded education only to those who participated in the founder's faith. The latter were for the worn out soldiers and sailors of the King who established them. Far be it from me to under-value these noble foundations—but I cannot help remarking that Sir Jamsetjee's benefactions with the sole exception I believe of the Parsee benevolent institution, are made to the entire community, not for Parsees only, but for Hindoos, Jews, Christians and Mahomedans.

"It is this Catholic character of Sir Jamsetjee's benevolence—his sympathy for the poor and suffering of all castes and creeds—that has won for him the universal respect and esteem of all classes of the Community, and it is to this feeling that we owe the gathering which the Sheriff's requisition has collected to-day in this hall. The manner in which Sir Jamsetjee Jeejeebhoy acquired his great wealth was hardly less honourable to himself and beneficial to the Community than the mode in which he dispenses it. By strict integrity, by industry and punctuality in all his commercial transactions, he has contributed to raise the character of the Bombay

Merchant in the most distant markets. His whole life is a practical illustration of the truth of the homely proverb—that "honesty is the best policy", and in this respect and in others he will leave behind him an example which I trust will long continue to be held up for imitation among us. But I have said enough, though certainly very far less than I might have said, upon Sir Jamsetjee Jeejeebhoy's claims upon our admiration and gratitude.

"I must not sit down without offering a few remarks upon the mode in which it is proposed that we should testify these sentiments. I hear that some object to a statue: it would be more consistent, they say, with the character of the man whom we seek to honour to make our tribute assume the shape of a work of charity than a work of art. I am unable to concur in this view. In the first place I would remark that Sir Jamsetjee has anticipated us in every work of charity with which we might seek to connect his name. We have already hospitals, Dhurumsallas, educational institutions, tanks, Causeways, and I know not how many other things, intended for the relief and instruction and convenience of the people called after him.

Besides I think we may well wish to perpetuate among the worthies who have a place in this Hall, or our public streets, the likeness of a man who has conferred such great benefits upon the Community and who will leave behind him so bright an example of all the qualities which dignify the acquisition of wealth and render its possession a blessing.

"More civilized nations both in ancient and modern times have adopted this mode of honouring distinguished public virtues and services. At Athens we read that the porticos were crowded with statues, and at Rome the number in the former became so great that the censor P. Cornelious Scipio and M. Papilius, removed all those which had not been erected with the sanction of the senate and the people. It is not likely that such an accumulation will take place anywhere in modern times—least of all is it likely in India; but if it were possible, I would venture to predict that no future censor would be found to direct the removal of the statue of Sir Jamsetjee Jeejeebhoy from the spot where it is to be placed, and that it will remain to distant generations a monument of the civic virtues of the Man, and of the gratitude of the Community."

The noble Lord sat down amidst cheers, and then as it were with the full assurance that his speech would meet with favour, the eloquent Mr. Anderson made the following excellent speech:—

"I feel that some apology is due from me for presenting myself to the meeting at so early a period of our proceedings. I may be permitted thus briefly to explain that, in undertaking to move this resolution, I have yielded to the opinion expressed to me, by several Native gentlemen, that my near relationship to one of his oldest friends would render my performance of this duty acceptable to Sir Jamsetjee Jeejeebhoy. It has been also indirectly intimated to me that a similar feeling was entertained by Sir Jamsetjee's sons. Under these circumstances, and having very much at heart the object for which this meeting was convened, I have felt that I ought not to shrink from the work which has been thus assigned to me. In this Hall we have frequently met to render our tribute of admiration to the heroes and statesmen who have illustrated the policy and the arms of our common country. This day we acquit ourselves of a duty dear to us all, of expressing our gratitude to one who, having acquired vast wealth by a long career of honorable industry, has distributed that wealth with unparalleled benevolence. The days are past when good deeds done in India remain unknown; this country is daily occupying a larger space in the minds of thoughtful men, and there is not a region on the civilized globe, from China to the far Republic of the West, which has not heard of the benevolent Knight of India. This island owes much to the public spirit of our Native fellow-citizens, it has enabled Bombay to maintain no unequal contest in the honorable emulation which progress must ever call forth between the three Presidencies. I believe that gentlemen who have devoted their best energies to the interests of Calcutta and Madras have said 'what could we not do if our Natives were like the Natives of Bombay.'

"Pre-eminent among those who have thus contributed to the prosperity of this Presidency is Sir Jamsetjee Jeejeebhoy. I fear that I should exhaust the patience of the meeting if I were to recount all the great public works which have been constructed by his munificence. I shall therefore only rapidly glance at some of the most prominent; but it ought not to be forgotten that, in addition to the great works which will endear his name to remote generations, his private— his almost secret charities have divided the weekly bread to thousands of his fellow creatures. The characteristic of his munificence has been enlightened usefulness.

"His wealth has beeen achieved by sagacity industry, and the purest good faith; it has not been lavished with mere ostentatious and ill considered profusion. In the long list of his public benefactions, there is not one which does not exhibit a wise discrimination, and amply deserve the title of a good work. Some have naturally been devoted to the relief and the improvement of the members of that ancient faith in which he was himself born and nurtured, but the greater portion have solely contemplated the common good of all. If a stranger landing on these shores were to inquire what were the works by which the Parsee Knight, of whom he had heard so much, had acquired his renown, we should but have to tell him 'to look around'. He would see Hospitals which, besides the tender offices they have extended to the afflicted, have, in conjunction with the Grant College, conferred on India the inestimable benefit of a skilled body of Native medical practitioners. He would see tanks, by which, to adopt the expression of Edmund Burke, 'the industry of man carefully husbands the precious gift of God.'. He would see, and not only here, but also at Nowsari in the North, and Khandallah in the South, Dhurumsallas—the homes of charity, in which the houseless and the wandering find refuge and relief. He would see the noble Causeway which unites the islands of Bombay and Salsette. He would see the water works at Poona, the bridges at Earla Parla and Bartha. He would see roads, wells, aqueducts and reservoirs.

"But these works, great as they are, are very far from representing all the good deeds of Sir Jamsetjee Jeejeebhoy. He has founded and endowed an institution for the education and maintenance of the children of poor Parsees, at an expense of nearly £ 50,000. Many of those whom I now address must have been present, as I was, when he gave in one gift to the sacred cause of Education the sum of £ 30,000; and they will not easily forget the sensation created by that announcement made with so much calmness and simplicity. But besides founding the schools which bear his name, and besides contributing most liberally to various other educational institutions, he has purposed to give a new impetus to the Native mind, to develop, if possible, another vein of talent by the formation of a school of design. To this great purpose he has devoted a sum of £s 10,000. But it would be to gild refined gold to dwell on the abundant evidences of the public spirit of this excellent citizen.

"It will be sufficient for me to repeat what has been said by the noble lord in the chair, that he has expended, for the solid and enduring benefit of Bombay, no less a sum than a quarter of a million sterling. But in addressing a meeting at which many of my own countrymen are present, I must not fail to allude to the facts that, when the bones of thousands of heroic men,— Europeans and Sepoys—were whitening in the snows of Cabool, when famine decimated the Highlands of Scotland, when a mysterious dispensation of Providence deprived our poor Irishmen of their daily food, when the widows and the orphans of the brave men who died for the right at Alma and Inkerman stretched forth their hands for aid, none evinced a more generous sympathy, none showed more alacrity in giving bread to the hungry, and binding up the wounds of the broken hearted, than he whom this day we honour ourselves in honoring. If, gentlemen, such deeds as these go without recognition in his own generation, the shame will be ours. The bloodless triumphs of Commerce have been illustrated by the noble names of Ashburton and Overstone. In the glorious temple which adorns the Capital of the British Empire in which lie, the bones of the iron victor of a hundred fields, and the mutilated form of him,—

"The saviour of the silver Coasted isle,
The shaker of the Baltic and the Nile;"

—in that temple near the marble which gives to posterity the form of Samuel Johnson, stands the statue of the illustrious philanthropist, John Howard. Nor could Learning and Valour demand a worthier associate. Let us then in the same spirit, give a great example to all India; let us show how a good man can be appreciated; and in this island, in which due reverence has been rendered to the genius of Wellesley and Elphinstone, to the virtues of Cornwallis and the gallant spirit of Malcolm, let us enable the humblest of his countrymen, in distant times, to gaze on the lineaments of their great benefactor. Such tributes are usually reserved for the illustrious dead. But in so mixed a population as that of Bombay, it is very meet that our venerable friend should know that all creeds and races, Parsees, Hindoos, Mussulmans, Jews and Christians have accorded to him their gratitude. That he should be assured by the concurrent voices of all, he has not laboured in vain, that he should see his good deeds, in the language of our great poet—

> "Formed in the applause
> Where they are intended, and which like an arch reverberates,
> The voice again, or like a gate of steel,
> Fronting the Sun, receives and renders back,
> His figure and his heat"

"He is now full of years. The evening of his days is brilliant with the lustre which anticipates the praises of posterity. Long may he "husband out life's taper at the close," happy in his most estimable family—happy in the applause and affection of his fellow citizens—happiest in the memory of his honorable and useful life."

Vociferous cheers followed this admirable speech, and it was then unanimously resolved that a statue should be erected to the memory of the first Knight of India, and placed in the Town

Hall. In 1860, a year after his death, the statue arrived. It bears the following inscription:—

SIR
JAMSETJEE JEEJEEBHOY
BARONET
1857. *

' A similar statue is now to be seen in the compound of that Gothic structure built by him for the relief of the sick, the hospital which bears his name.

All honour to those who joined in this most excellent project, for no better man could be found for the honour, as he was

> The pauper's friend, the rich man's peer,
> Beloved by all, both far, and near.

CHAPTER XI.

And now came a time when

> That India's Empress, England's Queen,
> That Queen of Queens, sedate, serene,
> That Queen of Albert's tender soul,
> Whose fame is heard from pole to pole,

Victoria, thought of once more honouring the man whom honour was due. Though his good works were a lasting monument of his glory and

---

* Really the inscription ought to be expressive of something more than the name and the year.

greatness, though the statue was sufficient "to point a moral or adorn a tale", yet works of art are subject to decay, and hence after a time, his name as well as the favours heaped on him by his Sovereign may be forgotten.

" The Knight-hood could not perpetuate his name to futurity, and seeing this, our beloved Sovereign now once more stretched her maternal hand to her brightest Indian subject. From a Knight she raised him to be a Baronet ! The catastrophe of' 57,

> "   That dreadful year,
> Which India did convulse,
> When Nana shook with rage and fear
> The British heart and pulse,

brought into prominence the till then latent feelings of loyalty in the hearts of the Parsees, foremost among whom was Sir Jamsetjee, who addressed to the Queen a letter couched in the most humble and loyal style, assuring her of the fidelity and affection of the sons of Zoroaster. This and some similar good offices of Sir Jamsetjee once more excited the admiration of his Sovereign, which resulted in the conferring of this noble title upon him in August, 1858. So long as India claims England for her Sovereign, so long this title will descend to posterity in the family of Sir Jamsetjee. And wise as he was in everything, there could not be a more prudent and thoughtful step than that he took on his being raised to the Baronetcy. To keep up the dignity of the future Sir Jamsetjees, he gave in one large amount the sum of twenty-five lacs of Rupees to Government, and caused a special act to be passed in the Legislative Council of India in the year 1860, that the future Sir Jamsetjees may receive from Government the interest for this amount at six per cent per annum for ever. A sum of nearly one lac of Rupees is thus payable every year to our present noble Baronet—Sir Cursetjee Jamsetjee Jeejeebhoy.

CHAPTER XII.

"Let the arrow leave the quiver,
It was fashion'd but to soar;
Let the waves pass from the river,
Into ocean ever more"

But apart from his public character and works which tell their own tale, let us now turn for a moment to his domestic life and then conclude this brochure.

As previously mentioned, Sir Jamsetjee married the lovely Avabye Framjee Bottlewalla at the age of sixteen. By her he had in all eight children, but of these four are dead, and the surviving are Setts Cursetjee (our present Baronet) Rustomjee, Sorabjee, and Bae Pherozbae.

Cursetjee was born on the 9th October 1811, and it is said that since his birth Sir Jamsetjee has been very successful and prosperous in his ventures. He now inherits the Baronetcy. In society he is an agreeable companion, and he is ever amongst the first to further a good object. He is an excellent speaker, and as chairman to various public meetings he has displayed an amount of knowledge and acumen which has been surpassed by few. By his recent trip to England he has acquired the polish of European refinement in his habits and manners which are wholly gentlemanly. A great lover of knowledge, he has endowed the Deccan with a magnificent building for the College at a cost of one lac of Rupees. He is ever among the foremost to promote any scheme that tends to the amusement of the Bombay public, being one of the earliest patrons of the Royal Italian Opera here, and of the theatrical corps of the Parsees which plays in English, and is known by the name of the "P. Elphinstone Club."

Rustomjee is the second child of Sir Jamsetjee and was born on the 23rd January 1824. In his temper, disposition and habits he is no way different from his illustrious father. Like him he is munificent to an extreme, and his purse is ever ready for all. Blessed like his noble father with an abundance of fortune, he freely gives what he has. Not a single fund, not a single subscription for any deserving object lacks his donation. Schools he has opened, Dharamsalas he has built, and temples he has supported. He is now a member of the Bombay Legislative Council. He is reserved in his habits, and unfortunately for us, on account of ill-health he is seldom or rarely to be seen in society. But however apart from the hum of the busy multitude, there is not a single request which passes by him unheeded. By his sound advice he has rescued many from ruin, and where money saves the character of a man, he is never backwards from proffering it.

The third son, Sorabjee (born 20th October 1825) is one of the few wealthy Natives who have devoted their lives to the closet. When fresh from school, he delivered some excellent lectures to the Natives on Morality. He is a great lover of the Oriental languages and a fair master of many of them. By his last trip to Gujarat he has done a great deal of good, and the poor city of Surat is promised a building for its school. Being himself a clever gentleman, he appreciates knowledge in others, and when opportunity offers he holds out a helping hand to them.

Sir Jamsetjee's daughter Bae Pherozebae (born 3rd January 1834) is a very amiable and clever woman. In features and stature she appears more an English than a Parsee lady. She is one of the very few native ladies who have been instructed in the language of our rulers. She writes and composes fairly, and though completely Native in her dress and style, her manners are wholly European.

Happy in such excellent children whose ambition was to rival each other in their obedience and affection towards their parents; happier in so good a wife, whose sole wish was to please her beloved in everything; and happiest of all in the little urchins, who as his

"Children's children, rode on his knee and heard his great watch tick"
the worthy Baronet's life's taper was burning to a close. The old Patriarch's race of glory was run. He had received honours which since the days of Saladin no Asiatic had acquired. And now comes the fatality. 'Midst the splendour around him he is now reclining. It is the solemn 15th of April 1859. We pass by his mansion in the Fort. An

JAMSETJEE'S APPROACHING END.

anxious look sits upon the faces of all, and they breathlessly await the result of the doctor's visit. Hushed and gentle are his footsteps as he leaves the sick man's room, for his message is pregnant with sorrow and his tidings are of death, For the noble heart is still for ever! Softly, calmly as the evening breeze was wafted over smooth waters of Backbay, beneath the pale grave face of the moon, he had passed to his eternal rest! The benefactor of his race and country, the master of nearly a thousand servants, the Jupiter of the Parsee Community, the greatest of the children of India, the noblest of the nobility of England, now sleeps the sleep of ages! Day broke serene and calm, and the mourners poured in. Hornby Row was crowded to excess, and from the Governor down to the street beggar, all came in to pay their last respects to the FIRST BARONET OF INDIA. The day was kept up in mourning by all classes in Bombay, and all the offices, banks and shops were closed to bemoan the loss of so great a man. His partner in life the venerable Lady Avabye survives, and worthily maintains among the female portion of the Parsee Community the position which her husband secured and always occupied among the whole of the Zoroastrian brotherhood.

CHAPTER XIII.

Scarcely is it necessary to recapitulate the domestic virtues of the object of this little memoir; they have been sufficiently developed already. As father, husband, friend, benefactor, call him what we will, his example among Asiatics is unique, to the world a brilliant model. Though a staunch adherent of the Zoroastrian faith, Jamsetjee's views were neither narrowly orthodox, nor obtrusively liberal, but nicely distinguishing the vital points of his religion from the shoals of error upon which less evenly balanced minds have made shipwreck. An ardent admirer of civilization in all its bearings, he was ever amongst the foremost in clearing away the mist of superstition which hung over the minds of his less enlightened countrymen. His loyalty towards his Sovereign and country was as constant and disinterested, as it was unquestionable and conspicuous, and his honesty and integrity were equally true and unassailable.

Unlike many Orientals Jamsetjee was ever faithful to the beloved partner of his joys and griefs, and his domestic virtues were ever free from taint or blemish. He was a kind and loving father to his children, by whom he was most tenderly and reciprocally beloved. In him as a friend all who confided their secrets to him trusted as a sure depository, knowing that their affairs would be kept under the lock and key of his heart. In his tastes and habits he was simple, in his address dignified and moderate. True retirement, the friend to old age, was his in his declining years, though to the last his ears were open to the requirements of his fellow creatures. "Steeped in poverty to the very deep" in his childhood, by patience and perseverance he was enabled to tread the way to Fortune. Heaven "tried him with affliction" when on the verge of enjoying that abundance which it had lavished upon him, but seeing him bear "the rain of sorrow" with such calm resignation, it stamped him as one "warranted" to withstand every shock from the fickle hands of Fortune. Long will it be ere his place be well supplied among the Parsee Community, although his second son, the Hon'ble Rustomjee Jamsetjee Jeejeebhoy bids fair to rival his father in generosity and acts of charity. But Jamsetjee was the one man, whom none ventured to oppose, whom all wished to love.

www.ingramcontent.com/pod-product-compliance
Lightning Source LLC
Chambersburg PA
CBHW022137160426
43197CB00009B/1321